~~No~~

Time

For

Anything

Live with Purpose, Master your Time

Craig D Robinson

You can contact the author at www.craigdrobinson.com

ISBN: 978-1533437020
Cover Design: Manisha Designs
Interior Design: Nicola Swankie
Publisher: CDR Publishers
Editor: Carrie Bean

1. Business 2. Time Management 3. Entrepreneurship
4. Management

Table of Contents

Introduction

Time flies.

Time is an illusion.

Time and tide wait for no one.

Have you noticed how time is often compared to something over which you have no control? It's become part of our conditioning to view time as a concept that is difficult to quantify.

Of course, we all have a watch or a clock to measure time but do we really make the most of our time?

Do you see time as a competitor in a race where it is always just a little bit ahead of you? Are you constantly running after time to do things, finish tasks and achieve something? Yet despite your best efforts, do you find yourself running out of time?

Do you envy and marvel at those who successfully manage to complete all their tasks on time while you are still playing catch-up?

Do you wish you had more than 24 hours in a day?

Well, you are not alone. Most people are leading busier lives than ever before. Yet they feel unfulfilled. In fact, people today spend more time at work than at any time in the last century.

So, does it mean that people are generally more productive because they spend more time working? Nope, in fact the level of satisfaction with life is lower than at any time in the last century.

Do you enjoy your time?

If a person spends time doing something they enjoy, then they feel that their time and efforts are worthwhile. If somebody spends their time and effort in an activity that they do not enjoy, they may feel like they are being productive, but are they still getting the same level of fulfilment or satisfaction?

Are you willing to spend time doing something you don't like? If your answer is no, then it seems like the majority of people disagree with you.

In fact, most people it seems, would prefer to spend time doing something they do not like and earn money than do something they enjoy and thereby earn less money or none at all.

They are choosing to work overtime and earn money rather than enjoy their time off by going to the beach or a movie. People are even taking fewer holidays than they used to and more often taking work with them when they do.

This doesn't mean however, that all leisure time needs to be unproductive nor does it mean that all the time spent working is unenjoyable.

As the old Confucian adage goes, "Find a job that you love and you will not have to work a day in your life". The happiness that you derive from any activity is integral to the value that is attached to it.

Reflect on your own life, are you trading your happiness to strive after perceived productivity?

How do we even measure productivity?

Productivity and efficiency are concepts that were developed as part of the industrial revolution, more than 100 years ago. Productivity then was measured in terms of the quantity or volume of results that were produced by a person or a group of people.

The intent was to produce more volume or quantity with fewer people and fewer man-hours spent in production.

Efficiency meant making the best use of the available resources to produce something. If you were able to achieve the same result with fewer resources than previously needed, then it indicated improved efficiency and therefore more profit.

People were expected to get better or more efficient as they became more experienced in a particular task. So, for instance, it may take 10 people 5 hours to produce a widget in the beginning.

After a few months or years, the same 10 people or a fewer number should be able to produce a widget in less than 5 hours. This would indicate that efficiency has improved and the productivity of the people has increased.

We can therefore say that efficiency and productivity were not linked to the value of the work involved, but rather on achieving the output as quickly as possible.

What does time mean to you?

It was predicted about a century back that people in developed countries would have more leisure time than ever before. It was estimated that an average person in economically advanced countries would work less than three hours a day.

Economists were also worried that there would be so much leisure time that it could become a potential problem because people would not know what to do with the time they had on their hands.

Take one look around you and you will know that none of these predictions or expectations was accurate. Most people are increasingly spending more time at work now than they did previously and it is definitely not anywhere near three hours a day.

Even when they are not at work, they are still able to work. Technology and media advancements have provided us with a surfeit of choices that always keep us connected and able to be contacted.

What does leisure mean?

The travel industry makes a very good distinction by defining any trip as either business or leisure. A business trip is about being productive and making money. A leisure trip is about pursuing our personal interests.

Most of our leisure activities involve socialising, hobbies or other mundane tasks such as eating, drinking, sleeping or physical activities such as walking, running or exercising. Most of these activities cost you money and even if they do not, they can rarely be said to be productive in the sense that you produce any money or measurable value by doing these activities.

Technological progress, advancements in industries and in the way we conduct business should all have led us to become less rushed and more relaxed. Yet when we look at our own lives or at the people around us, we notice that most of us are always in a hurry to do something or busy doing something; in fact the advancements in technology have actually meant that the sanctuary of leisure time has become increasingly disrupted and now we are all too often still checking emails on family holidays.

Whether we call it work or pleasure, business or leisure or productive versus non-productive activities, it is a matter of choice. We can choose to be continually busy or we can choose to disconnect and make the most of our time and be happy.

So is this book about time management?

Yes and no. It is about time management in the sense that it tells you how you can make the most of your time doing activities that you enjoy.

However, the broader lesson is why it is so crucially important not to fill your life only with activities that are productive; it will teach you how to make the choice.

There is an anecdote that demonstrates how productivity or success differs according to a person's viewpoint.

A successful businessman was on holiday in a remote and picturesque fishing village. At the pier, he met a local fisherman who had docked his boat after catching some fish. It was quite early in the day, so the businessman asked the fisherman why he had returned from sea.

The fisherman replied that he had caught enough fish to sell and fulfil his and his family's needs.

The businessman asked what he would do the rest of the day. The fisherman replied that he would enjoy a delicious lunch with his family, have an afternoon siesta, go for a stroll in the evening and then enjoy a glass of wine or two before dinner.

The businessman told him that he could show the fisherman how to become more successful. He should go back to sea and catch more fish and then use the extra money to buy more boats with which he can catch even more fish.

He could also sell the fish in other parts of the country or even anywhere in the world by processing, packing and exporting fish.

Success is a matter of perception.

The fisherman nodded to all this and then asked what the point of all this was? The businessman was surprised that the fisherman did not see the point and replied that it was about becoming more successful by being more productive.

The fisherman then asked how long it will take to be successful. The businessman replied that it would depend on how hard the fisherman was willing to work and how much of his time he was willing to spend. He said it would perhaps take a few years to become successful.

The fisherman wanted to know what he would gain once he was successful. The businessman thought about it for a while and then said that it would give him more time to enjoy life. The fisherman wanted to know how he could enjoy life.

The businessman said that he could spend more time with his family, do what he wanted, relax and enjoy a glass of wine whenever he wanted.

The fisherman thought about it and asked why he should work hard and wait many years to do what he enjoyed doing instead of doing it right now? After all, he was already enjoying life.

Can you do more and still enjoy life?

Time has been likened to many things: the sands sifting through an hourglass; a circus that is always packing up and moving away; an arrow moving straight and swiftly forward, or a river that is constantly flowing.

The main problem with most of these metaphors? They create the impression that you cannot control time. That time moves on no matter what.

The secret to having a productive and fulfilling life?

Understanding you can control time. That it is something real and tangible.

Your time is precious and it's yours. Make a commitment to yourself to no longer accept that your time will just drain away; it is absolutely within your power to do so much more with it.

If you can be conscious and take care of your time, it will serve you well in return.

Who is this book for?

This book is for every person who wants to make the most of their time. It is for the entrepreneur, the businessperson, the employee, the artist, the dreamer and the doer who want to make their life not just productive but more fulfilling and meaningful. It is for those who want not only to do more with their life but to enjoy doing so.

How does it work?

It will take you through a number of methodologies that will help you master a powerful mindset about what can be achieved with your time, and practical tips on how to ensure you are being conscious and actively aware of how you spend your time throughout your day to ensure you get the most from it.

1. Your time is not yours alone.

You are not the only person in your life.

You have goals; you also have various communities you belong to that are a key part of your identity. Whether it is a family, your workmates, your local sports club, a volunteer organisation or simply socialising with a group of friends.

When you allocate your time, you need to take into account all that is part of you. Your needs, your goals and the people who matter to you. Taking great care not to ignore or neglect any aspect of your life. In fact, if we neglect or borrow time away from important aspects of our lives, it has a habit of demanding that time back from us, often at the most inconvenient time.

This includes your own rest and relaxation.

Find the right balance.

Are you so engrossed in your work that you neglect your health? Are you so busy with work that it is difficult to find some time to spend with your family and friends?

It's only for a short while, you say. If I work hard now, then I will be able to achieve my goals sooner, and later, I can find the time to indulge.

There are millions of people who say this and they find out too late that life has passed them by.

Then there are the successful few who live complete and fulfilled lives. They are healthy, happy and have time for their personal passions, hobbies, their family and friends, and also work hard to achieve success in their professional lives.

Your goals are important.

Whether they are financial, career- or business-related, your goals help you focus on what is important to you and where you want to be in the immediate future as well as some years from now. These goals should not exclude the rest of your life; goals like how much time you spend with your family, and personal pursuits are equally important and should not be ignored.

Life happened.

This is what Eve, a childhood friend, told me when I met her, many years later at a school reunion. After we talked about our respective careers, our families, the places we went to on holidays and the escalating real estate prices, the conversation naturally turned to her great talent for music.

She had been part of the local choir when we were in school and then later, when she was in college she had played the piano semi-professionally at concerts, social occasions and functions as well as every Tuesday at a very popular jazz bar and restaurant.

In fact, the succulent steaks they served at the place vied for attention with the exquisite music that Eve played. It was no secret that to get a reservation on any Tuesday, you had to book well in advance.

I asked her if she still played the piano. "Do you think I have time for that?" she laughed and said, "When I am not busy at work then I am with my kids and two hours later, I wish I was back at work."

I could see from the way her fingers fluttered over imaginary keys in the air, that she missed music. It had once been a defining passion of hers.

"What happened? You had so much talent," I said.

"Life happened," she said.

That's when it hit me: the regret, the sense of loss and the longing that she felt for the absence of music in her life. It was clearly evident in her eyes even though she refused to admit it in actual words.

You are responsible.

Whether you are an entrepreneur or an employee, you have to remember one crucial fact. You are responsible for your life and your time. You cannot and should not expect your employer, the government, your personal assistant or any other external entity, to help you achieve work-life balance.

Your life belongs to you. You have the responsibility to live your life the way you want to. You can't just let life happen.

You belong in a group, a family, a circle of friends and well-wishers. They are your responsibility and you need to make time to maintain your relationship with them.

Your goals belong to you. You have a responsibility not only for creating them but also for pursuing them. You don't just dream, you follow your dreams.

If you don't, they will follow you and haunt you. Before you realise it they will have withered and turned into ghosts or regrets.

Just like a plant, your goals and ambitions need to be cared for and nurtured.

You can't do it all in one day.

What's your ideal day like? Does it involve going to the gym, having breakfast with your family, working hard at your business or job, playing golf, coffee with friends and watching the sunset at the beach?

There is so much you want to do and there is only so much time. You want to do so many things all at once. You realise that there are only 24 hours in a day.

You don't have to do it all in one day.

That's why there are weekdays and weekends. Most of us call them workdays and holidays.

Successful people simply call them days of their lives or days that are for living. Each day is worth your time and if you know how, then you can derive value from every day of your life.

There is no rule that says you cannot take a day off on a weekday or a workday to go to the beach.

Similarly, there is no reason why you should not work on a Sunday if you want to, but not necessarily because you have to.

The important thing to remember is that only you are responsible for what you do on any given day. You are responsible for the hours you spend at work or don't spend, and also for the holidays you take or don't take.

Fill your life with meaningful moments.

Creating value does not necessarily mean being highly productive but it does mean finding meaning and purpose, love and happiness. In other words, it is about finding the right balance.

You may not be able to do it every day but over a week, or over a month or a few months, you can find the right balance.

You will know that you have achieved work-life balance when you are eager to go to work, but at the same time are not too tired after work to spend time with your family.

You are (and should be) happy to spend a day at the museum or an evening at the movies without feeling guilty because you know that you've worked hard and deserve to live your life.

You have a whole life to do everything. The trick is to distribute the activities in such a manner that you do not neglect your needs, both personal and professional. Nurture your goals whether they are career-oriented, business-related, financial, personal, professional or social concerning your family and friends.

Think about each aspect of your life. Then make a commitment to yourself, your goals and the people who matter to you.

Take a piece of paper and divide it into three columns: one for you, one for your goals and one for your relationships.

Now write down activities that come under each category. You have a commitment to your health and wellbeing. So you need to find the time to exercise, not just your body but your mind and soul.

What are your goals? Include professional as well as personal ones. Then allocate the time to pursue them. Make time for the people who matter in your life.

None of these activities should seem like you are duty bound to do them but they should come joyfully and naturally. You will realise as you read this book that you have all the time you want in your life and you can make the most of it, right here, right now.

2. Start. Now.

There is no such thing as a good time or a bad time. There is simply time.

When it comes to time, the past and the future are not as relevant or important as the present. What you are doing now is most important.

What you plan to do next or what you did yesterday doesn't matter as much as what you are doing right now.

An athlete or sportsperson is only as good as the race he is running now or the game he is playing now. His performance in the last race or game is as irrelevant as the next one.

This applies to you whoever you are, whether you are a pianist or a plumber, an employee or an entrepreneur. Your current actions, work and performance and the results that they produce are what makes you real, alive and relevant.

Your actions in this moment, right here right now, define who you are and what you represent.

Perhaps you did something well in the past and that's great. It does not mean that you can live the rest of your life not trying to do something even better or different.

Similarly, if you are planning to do something which you are sure you will succeed in, it still doesn't have any meaning or value until you actually start doing it.

Don't sabotage your success.

If there is one sure way to fail, it is to delay doing something.

Procrastination or putting off things is believed to be the number one reason why people fail. Procrastination has been called the enemy of productivity and the thief of time, and rightly so.

It is estimated that about 20% of people, from business leaders to executives, students to seasoned professionals, put off performing some tasks till the last minute. Why?

It's the habitual response or condition that a person develops over a period of time. People who delay doing things are usually compulsive or repeat procrastinators. They could be delaying doing something intentionally for any number of reasons.

When it's habitual, more often than not, the person doesn't even realise that they are delaying something. This is how they live their lives.

What's worse than doing something wrong?

Not doing anything at all.

Don't do it if you can't do it right. This is what a procrastinator will tell himself or herself in order not to do something.

They say they are planning and think that they are waiting for the perfect moment when they will have all the information or resources necessary to complete a task.

While this may seem like a perfectionist attitude, and it often is, but it is still a flaw or handicap which can prevent a person from being happy, productive or successful.

Life is simply not geometrical. You cannot draw a perfectly straight line or a perfectly round circle. Things are unpredictable, asymmetrical and irregular.

The first wheels that were made with human hands and primitive tools were not perfectly round. Yet they worked as wheels even though the journey was a little slower and bumpier.

It took thousands of years before sophisticated machines were invented and the perfectly round wheel was made to ensure a smoother and faster journey.

If you don't connect the dots, you cannot see the picture. Perfectionism in a person can easily become a drawback instead of an advantage, if it promotes procrastination. Accept imperfection in yourself and the tasks you complete. Done is better than perfect.

Closing your eyes doesn't mean it isn't there.

People procrastinate intentionally when they do not want to face the consequences. They think that they can be blamed only if they try to do something and fail. If they don't even try, then nobody will ever know about their failure.

Procrastinators who put off doing things intentionally are behaving like the proverbial ostrich that hides its head in the sand to avoid danger.

It's a foolish response because it only makes the task seem more difficult than it really is. It also erodes the person's confidence progressively with every act of procrastination.

Fear of failure is just as much a reason to procrastinate as fear of success. Some people may deliberately put off performing certain actions because they are afraid of success.

You may find this difficult to believe or understand but it is a real and valid reason to procrastinate.

Success often brings with it more responsibilities and therefore more chances of failure in the future.

People who procrastinate intuitively realise that taking some steps means committing to a long journey. If they delay taking that first step, then they can pretend that they do not have to go on the journey at all.

You can overcome procrastination.

The good news is that procrastination is not an inherent personality trait. Procrastinators are not born that way. They become so or are made that way by their environment or their own predilections for getting things right and avoiding failure at all costs.

If you are working with too many distractions, then you are in the perfect environment to turn into a procrastinator. A cluttered or disorganised workplace or the lack of a disciplined or systematic approach to tasks can lead to procrastination.

Here are a few tips to avoid and overcome procrastination.

- Find out why you are putting off doing something.

Once you know the reason, it is easy to overcome it. Are you not doing it because you hate doing it or because you think it is not important? Or are you afraid you might fail? Is it because of a lack of focus or an inability to get your priorities right?

- Get rid of distractions.

Your environment can explain why you are more prone to inaction than action. It could be a messy desk or room or it could be a noisy fan or an open door or window. It could also be people, colleagues or friends who feed your fears and distract you from the task at hand.

- Plan for just 5 minutes and then stop.

This is a sensible method to break procrastination that masquerades as planning. The logic behind it is that there is very little worth planning for more than 5 minutes as you cannot improve your actions by prolonging the planning stage. This makes you start doing something now rather than doing it later.

- Set a timeline to do or finish something.

Procrastinators tend to linger on or tinker around doing a particular activity so that they do not have to move on to the next stage or next action. It is not only important to start something on time but also to finish it. When you set a deadline for a task, there's less tendency to delay it. Even if you don't finish it, move on to something else and come back to the task later.

- Reward yourself.

This is self-explanatory. You can motivate yourself to do something which you consider either unpleasant or something which you are afraid of, by promising yourself a reward for doing it. Your reward could be something as simple as a cup of coffee when you complete the task or the opportunity to do a activity that you love.

Finally, remember that every time you say 'not now' or 'later', you are dilly-dallying and allowing time to slip through your fingers and fly away.

3. Write your 'not-to-do' list.

Most of us know the importance of writing a to-do list. It is generally considered to be the most important productivity tool.

Writing a to-do list has been known to dramatically improve productivity and enable people to get more done in less time. Yet, in spite of scrupulously writing a to-do list every day and following it, do you still find yourself spending more time at work than you want to?

Then it is time to create a 'not-to-do' list.

Think of all the things that you do in a typical day, which are preventing you from completing the tasks on your to-do list.

These could be any activities that either distract you from being productive, consume too much of your time and can be delegated, or are simply unnecessary but you do them out of habit.

Get rid of the thieves who steal your time.

So a hypothetical daily 'not-to-do' list may contain items such as these:

- Do not check your email inbox during certain periods.
- Do not visit social networking sites during certain periods.
- Do not take more than x number of coffee or tea breaks.

- Do not answer or make calls during certain periods.
- Do not schedule or attend meetings on certain days of the week.

Do you get the general idea? On the surface of it, avoiding these activities may seem really simple and easy but it isn't.

How many times have you picked up the phone to hear someone tell you it will only take a few minutes? Then before you even realise it, 20 minutes or even an hour or more has passed by the time you put the phone down.

It's the same with checking or answering your emails or browsing the internet.

Find the hidden flaws in the big picture.

There are certain activities which seem so small that you think that they will only take a few minutes. These minutes add up over days, weeks or even months, and eventually these small bits of time become so big that they eat into your productive time.

It's easy to spot the time thieves that occur on a daily basis as we just saw, but what about those occasional recurring activities? These are the ones which you do not come across every day but they still happen on a regular basis albeit less frequently.

Consider activities like meeting clients, attending seminars, conducting reviews or evaluating proposals. You may be performing these activities once in a while and you think that they cannot be avoided.

Or can they be? Is there someone else who can do them?

If so, delegate.

Perhaps there's another way of doing them?

Are you commuting long distances in order to meet clients? If so, can these meetings be done via a video conference call?

Are you conducting reviews or evaluating proposals because you've always done them? Isn't it time that someone else took over?

This is especially important if your job description has changed because you got promoted. Or can the responsibility be rotated among your co-workers in the team so each member gets the opportunity to do it?

The occasional yet recurring time-wasters are not as obvious as those that happen on a daily basis. You may need to spend some time thinking over and considering what you've been doing repeatedly which can be avoided or delegated.

Go over your to-do lists for the last six months or a year and identify the recurring activities which you can eliminate, delegate or modify. Then make a 'not-to-do' list which includes all these.

Ideally, you should have two 'not-to-do' lists: a micro one which details the daily time-wasting activities to be avoided and a macro list which identifies the latent time-wasting activities which lie hidden within your larger weekly, monthly or annual schedule.

A 'not-to-do' list for your to-do list.

Making a to-do list is easy. Making it work for you isn't.

To make your to-do list more effective, avoid these common pitfalls:

- Don't make it too long.

  One of the most likely reasons your to-do list isn't working for you is because you are attempting to do too much. Does your to-do list look like a grocery receipt? If yes, then you could be stretching yourself too thin.

  Ideally a daily to-do list should not contain more than nine items. Why nine and not 10?

  Well, you may occasionally have 10 or even 11 or more but try to limit it to 9 or fewer items because it's easier to remember and follow. It's the same reason why a billboard slogan which contains 9 or fewer words is more memorable than one which has a longer message.

- Do not leave your list open-ended.

Is your to-do list clear? Do you know when an item on the list is done or completed? You need to qualify each item with a specific end result or outcome so that it can be ticked off as completed.

For instance, if you are following up with a client or customer for non-payment, then is your action item completed by just making a call? Or does it involve ensuring you have a definite date when the cheque will be sent or the fund transfer made?

- Keep your list where you can see it, don't let it get covered by less important paperwork

This may seem highly improbable but you'll be surprised how often it happens. Make sure you have access to it at all times. You may have typed it out on your phone or tablet and the battery dies. What do you do? Can you remember it?

This does not necessarily mean that you have to always write it on a piece of paper but sometimes old-school techniques trump technology.

- Do not forget to prioritise.

Every item on your list should have a number assigned to it indicating its importance. You cannot attempt to do them randomly.

You should categorise them according to what you absolutely must do that day and what you can afford to carry over to the next day in case you can't accomplish all of them.

- Do not let any item hog your time.

Assign a specific amount of time to each task. This way you will be able to quantify the correct number of tasks you can do within a day. It will also prevent you from spending more time than is necessary on any one task or more time than that task deserves. Be clear how important the outcome is and how much of your life you are willing to devote to achieving that outcome.

- Do not write your to-do list in the morning.

Write it the night before. Why? So that you can plan well in advance and not start your day by spending time deciding what to do or prioritising the items.

When you do it the night before, not only will you get a good night's rest but you are already prepared to start doing something when the day starts instead of merely planning. This is an especially important way to make the most of your time and you'll discover in detail how you can do so in the next chapter.

4. Schedule your day the night before.

When you look at the habits of productive people, you will notice that most of them are early risers. No wonder, several studies point to getting up early as one of the key ingredients to achieving success.

However, what they fail to realise is that getting up early is only part of the story. The importance of sleeping on time, sleeping well and simply sleeping are often ignored.

There is so much emphasis on rising an hour earlier to get more things done that most people generally spoil their sleep so that they can get up earlier. Not only is this unhealthy but it is also counter-productive.

If you don't sleep well or long enough, you are going to be groggy and grumpy and in no condition to accomplish anything.

How much sleep is enough varies from person to person but generally seven to nine hours' sleep every night is considered essential.

What's all this got to do with productivity or making the most of your time, you may be wondering.

Productivity has more to do with sleep than you thought or possibly even imagined.

Right your rhythm.

We often talk about having 24 hours in a day but do you realise that actually there are far fewer than 24 hours in a day? In fact, there is only about half that number of hours in any given day because the rest of the hours make up what we know as night or sleeping time.

Of course, there are days when you burn the proverbial midnight oil in an attempt to get more things done. So you keep awake and don't sleep until late at night.

You will then set an alarm to wake you up because you know that you cannot predict when you will wake up especially after a late night.

Then when you wake up, whether it is late or whether it is early or at the same time as you usually do, you will still find that you are not your usual self when you wake up.

You will not generally feel refreshed even if you have slept more than you usually do. Why does this happen?

It's because you have upset your circadian rhythm. Also referred to as your internal body clock, the circadian rhythm is governed by the sun or the presence of light during the day and darkness during the night.

You wake up only when you sleep.

It is the reason why we suffer from jet lag when we travel, or why people who work night shifts take a long time to adjust their sleeping patterns.

It could also be the reason why cases of clinical depression or insomnia occur more during the winter. Clinical depression is also more common in cold places where, during the winters, the days generally start out as dull and dreary because there is less morning sunlight.

If sleep can influence your day so much, then isn't it important that we devote some time to it?

You can either plan for your day the previous night or you can plan for it when you wake up.

Count sheep before you sleep.

The main advantage of planning the next day the night before is that you sleep well because you have squared away all your concerns before hitting the bed. Never go to bed without resolving an argument is an oft-repeated marriage counselling advice for the same reason.

There are things you can prepare for in the morning and there are things you can prepare for at night before you go to sleep.

A highly successful athlete attributed his consistent performance to the simple habit of putting out his playing gear, outfit and shoes the previous night. He said that it helped him to get a good night's sleep because he wasn't worried that he would have to spend time looking for them in the morning.

In myths and fables, the act of imagining sheep jumping over a fence and counting them is known to induce sleep. Another alternative is to count the stars.

Similarly, I have found it extremely beneficial by preparing my to-do list or filling out what I call my Daily Priority Sheet (DPS) before I go to sleep. It is better than counting sheep and more effective.

I have attached a sample of the Daily Priority Sheet for your reference at the end of this chapter.

Knowing what I have to do the next day and knowing that I have prepared for and allocated the time for each task is a wonderfully easy and effective way to go to sleep and wake up refreshed.

Things that don't go bump in the night.

Do you know why reading a horror story or watching a horror movie at night is scarier than doing so during the day?

There is a reason why the creators of imaginary scary creatures like monsters, parasites or zombies associate them with the night.

There is also a reason why most of these creatures become sluggish or less potent during the day in these myths or stories.

In fact, most people whose hair stands on end when they read a horror story or watch a horror movie at night will pooh-pooh the very idea of monsters or parasites in broad daylight.

A lot of things happen during the night and it's not just imaginary creatures hiding in the closet or under our beds. Our circadian rhythm is tuned by the secretion of a hormone called melatonin.

In a healthy person, melatonin is secreted when it gets dark and the person gets ready to sleep. While the person is sleeping, melatonin is working hard to replenish your body.

It is a powerful antioxidant and aids in cleansing the toxins accumulated during the day's activities in your body.

It also relaxes your muscles and mind, and influences essential functions within the body such as the digestive process and blood circulation.

Even in people with high blood pressure, it has been observed that when they sleep their blood pressure levels become normal.

Have you observed how sometimes you feel a bit colder at midnight or in the pre-dawn when you wake up? It's because melatonin has been working to regulate the blood flowing to your arms and legs so that they can relax.

In fact, if you do not feel a bit cold when you wake up after sleeping, it could be a warning sign that your body is not producing enough melatonin. It also means that your sleep has not been restful.

This is one of the reasons why people have insomnia.

Insufficient production of this hormone can also cause other health complications. Studies have indicated that the incidence of certain types of cancer is more pronounced among people who work night shifts or have irregular sleeping and waking patterns.

The bedtime story.

Darkness while you sleep and exposure to light during the day are essential for the production of melatonin. The reverse is also true.

Getting some sunlight in the morning is also important for the production of melatonin at night.

Turning off the TV or not watching it or using your computer just before you sleep can help you sleep better. The light emanating from the TV screen or your computer monitor tells your body it is still daytime and your melatonin production stays at a daylight level. It typically takes at least an hour for your body to switch over to a night rhythm once daylight or harsh screen light dims.

Similarly, reading a book in bed is likely to help you sleep better than watching TV in your bedroom.

In my experience, preparing for your next day the night before is not only a good practice but also an effective way to improve your productivity.

If you still think that you'd rather plan for the day in the morning, I suggest you look at and learn from children.

Children like to be read bedtime stories. Ever tried telling a child that you will read the story in the morning?

Our mind and body needs to be assured that all's well so that it doesn't have to worry about any doubts which may turn into monsters. Tasks that are not planned for the next day can easily disturb your sleep by becoming no less menacing than a monster lurking in dark corners at night.

Filling the Daily Priority Sheet is one way to put your mind to rest.

DAILY PRIORITY SHEET

Name: Date:

Who do I need to contact today?   Who am I waiting to hear from?

_____   _____

_____   _____

_____   _____

_____   _____

_____   _____

_____   _____

_____   _____

PRIORITIES

1. _____

2. _____

3. _____

4. _____

5. _____

6. _____

7. _____

8. _____

9. _____

10. _____

5. A tomato, now and then will get things done.

Did you walk up the stairs today? If so, did you count how many steps you took to climb the stairway?

If your answer was yes to the first question and no to the second one, then we can safely assume that you are of reasonably healthy body and mind.

Alright, jokes apart, stairs are a great metaphor to demonstrate the effectiveness of taking breaks in between tasks.

Just as I used a joke to break the monotony of a serious stretch of thoughts and ideas about time management, breaking down your daily schedule into ideal lengths of time for work-related activity interspersed with rest or relaxation to refuel and recover your energy and focus is a proven way to consistently accomplish more and improve your productivity.

Phew! Didn't you find it tiresome to read that long sentence?

Don't worry. It is the longest you'll ever encounter in the whole book. I am deliberately using it to demonstrate another relevant point here.

It is difficult to sustain your energy and concentration for long periods of time. Reading a long sentence can tax your thought process so much that you fail to follow its meaning. Conversely, it is easier to read and understand shorter sentences than a longer one.

Why do it the hard way?

Which is easier to climb, a stairway or a mountain? If somebody built a stairway along the side of Mount Everest, I bet there would be more people scaling the summit than ever.

Unfortunately, building a stairway on the face of a mountain is not just difficult but next to impossible.

As any building professional or engineer will tell you, building stairways require more time, effort and resources than say, building walls or floors.

Why do we go to all the trouble to build stairs? Why not just build a slope at an appropriate incline?

The answer, of course, is because climbing stairs is easier than climbing an incline. Otherwise it's not much different than climbing a mountain.

Similarly, taking short breaks throughout your schedule has been known to remarkably increase productivity.

Divide your day.

When you run a marathon, you will come across refreshment stops at designated points along the route which offer water and refreshments. If you look at the run routes of different marathons, you will discover that these stops occur more or less at similar distances.

Do you know that most marathon runners don't refer to a marathon as a race? Instead they prefer to call it a run. You may wonder if there is even a difference between a race and a run. There is, although it's a very subtle one.

In a race, the emphasis is on speed. In a marathon, the emphasis is on completing the run. That's why, when you are in a race, you cannot afford to stop because speed is of the essence.

However, when you run a marathon, taking those breaks to hydrate or taking a breather can actually prevent you from tiring yourself out. So that you have the stamina to go on and on to complete the long distance.

In other words, a marathon is nothing but a series of short sprints. This doesn't mean that timing isn't important in a marathon. It is, but it is secondary to completing the run.

After all, what's the point in running faster than everyone for the first 10 miles and then losing steam and stamina so that you fail to finish?

Treat every day as a marathon. Focus on completing the task or tasks at hand. You will automatically get more done.

The Pomodoro Effect

We live in an age where there are plenty of apps that promise to help you improve your productivity. You will be interested to know that a key principle on which many of these apps are based was developed in the 1980s by an Italian entrepreneur named Francesco Cirillo.

Have you heard of the Pomodoro Technique for productivity? If you have, or if you speak Italian, you may, by now, have guessed why tomatoes were mentioned in the title of this chapter.

Pomodoro is Italian for tomato. The productivity technique is named after a tomato-shaped kitchen timer that Cirillo used to break down his time and schedule.

He achieved peak productivity by taking short breaks at regular intervals. These productivity periods, he called Pomodori, which is the plural of Pomodoro.

The best thing about the Pomodoro Technique is that it is very simple and easy to implement. All you need is a simple kitchen timer device such as the one used to time baking a cake, boiling eggs or cooking pasta.

5 points to improve your productivity.

The Pomodoro Technique works simply because it doesn't make any great demand of effort or time. Instead it asks you to follow a disciplined approach to productivity.

The whole process can be explained in 5 simple points.

1. Pick a task from your to-do list.
2. Set the timer for 'n' number of minutes.
    (How many minutes is ideal? Cirillo recommends 25 minutes but you can choose between 25-50 minutes. I will talk about the ideal period for sustained productivity in another chapter, later in this book.)
3. Work on the task for the allocated time. If you finish the task, then tick a box against the task in your to-do list. If you don't complete the task, stop when the timer goes off.
4. Take a short break. (Cirillo recommends 5 minutes.) You may return to the task after the break or take up another task.
5. After 4 Pomodoris or productivity periods, take a longer break. (15 to 30 minutes.)

What do you do during the breaks? Get up and stretch. Go for a short walk. Make a cup of coffee or tea. Sip some water. Meditate. Take deep breaths. It's entirely up to you. The idea is to rest, relax and go back to work feeling refreshed.

The important aspect of the Pomodoro Technique is discipline. You should not allow interruptions of any kind during productivity periods.

You should also not prolong a productivity period after the timer goes off. You stop right away and then take a break. You pick up where you stopped after the break.

You continue doing this until you can tick the task off your list. The technique works for almost all types of work.

It is especially favoured by designers, developers, artists and writers, or professionals engaged in creative work or craft.

This could perhaps be because the breaks give you the space and time to review or make course corrections. It can therefore contribute not only to productivity but better quality of workmanship.

Go digital or mechanical.

The inventor of the Pomodoro Technique, Francesco Cirillo preferred a mechanical timer. He felt that the physical act of manually winding up the timer after each Pomodori or productivity period is significant.

However, for all practical purposes, you can use a digital app on your phone, tablet or computer. While using apps are convenient, there is no harm in using an actual tomato-shaped kitchen timer in honour of the developer.

Not only will it add colour to your desk, you may even find it inspiring. After all, it will cost you next to nothing and the returns could be improved productivity forever.

6. Replace your routines with rituals.

"I'll start working on it once I clear my inbox. I got more than a 100 emails over the weekend."

"I've been meaning to work out. It's just that I haven't got an empty slot in my tight schedule."

"There are a dozen things on my mind. I don't even know where to begin."

I am sure you have heard these words at some point or another. Let's try to describe in two words what these people are doing—making excuses.

That's right. They are making excuses because they are bogged down by routine.

A mentor of mine once told me that the main difference between productive people and the rest is that the former create rituals while the latter follow routines.

It took me a while to figure out the difference between a routine and ritual.

Routines are boring, dull, mindless, tedious tasks that you do because you've always done them or because you are expected to do them.

Let's consider some examples of routine behaviour: brushing your teeth, taking a shower or drinking a cup of coffee when you wake up in the morning.

Checking your emails or attending meetings are no different. You are not thinking about their relevance or significance.

You are just doing them. You are not even sure if you enjoy doing any of these chores, are you? For that matter, you may not even be thinking whether doing any of these really matters or makes any difference to your life.

Go from mindless to meaningful.

The Russian music composer, Tchaikovsky, went for a two-hour walk every day, without fail. The Swedish movie maker, Ingmar Bergman slept for an hour in the afternoon, regularly, no matter how busy his schedule.

Hemingway used to begin his writing as the sun rose while Franz Kafka did not begin writing until 11 o'clock in the evening. Of course, Kafka had a day job following which he slept in the evening for a few hours and woke up to have dinner only after which his creative pursuits began.

David Carp, founder of Tumblr is known to read and reply to his emails only in the morning between 9 and 10 am, not before or later.

Kenneth Chennault, CEO of American Express, makes a list at the end of every day where he writes down 3 things that he is going to accomplish the next day.

Arianna Huffington, founder of Huffington Post starts every morning with 30 minutes of meditation.

Despite the different things that all these people did or do on a daily or regular basis, one common trait that binds them is the fact that they are all highly successful. They are prolific in their work, consistently productive and generally considered to live or have lived fulfilling lives.

They produced not only large volumes of great work but did so in a consistent manner. They are definitely role models that we can emulate if we want to be successful or productive.

What you will discern here are acts of conscious choice that these people made. They did not do any of these things out of force of habit but out of a deliberate desire to improve their lives.

This is what differentiates a ritual from a routine. A ritual is a meaningful action which is done because the person who does it derives pleasure and also has a sense of being engaged in the action.

Change yourself and you can change the world.

Benjamin Franklin began every day with the question, "What good shall I do this day?" and ended every day with another question, "What good have I done today?"

"Every morning I asked myself, if today were the last day of my life, would I want to do what I am about to do today? Whenever the answer is no, then I know I need to change something."

This is what Steve Jobs said in a talk he gave at Stanford University.

How many questions like these do we ask and how often?

A routine repeatedly confronts you, and you give into it thereby leaving no room for improvement. Einstein said that insanity is doing the same thing over and over again, and expecting different results.

If you are going to be constantly occupied with checking and replying to emails, then how can you expect to build a business?

Are you busy working in your business when you should be working on your business?

Is the major part of your time spent sitting through long meetings? Are you gainfully using the time you spend stuck in traffic while commuting to and from work?

Are you working late at night and therefore oversleeping? Do you rush through your mornings and therefore have no time for breakfast?

If you are in so big a rush that you skip the most important meal of the day, then how will you find the time to ask yourself any meaningful questions?

How can you even consider 30 minutes of meditation in the morning, if you don't even have 3 minutes to contemplate your life?

Start smart.

A ritual is repetitive but unlike a routine, it transforms you. With a routine you are stuck in a rut. With a ritual, you experience the freedom of doing something out of choice.

Routines prevent you from doing the things that really matter. Rituals present you with opportunities to change the way you see things, do things and live your life.

Rituals are smart. Routines are not.

You may already be doing some things right when you feel inspired, which produces great results intermittently. The key is to identify these things and then convert them into daily or weekly rituals so you can reap their benefits on a regular basis.

What time of the day are you the most productive?

People have different personalities and though studies indicate that most successful people have productive morning rituals, it is important to find out what works best for you.

Some people may start their day as early as 4 am while others may not wake up until 7 am. Some may prefer to do their most important work in the morning while others will find the afternoons more suitable for productivity.

The important thing is to explore your personality, experiment with different approaches, take notes and keep records. Eventually, you'll be able to evolve a daily ritual that reads something like this:

7 am	Wake up and go for a walk
7:45 am	Breakfast
8-9:30 am	Work (Best time to work)
9:30-10:30 am	Read letters
10:30 am-12 noon	Work
12 noon	Walk the dog
12:25 pm	Lunch
3 pm	Rest, read
4 pm	Walk
4:30-5:30 pm	Work, clear up for the day
6 pm	Rest, read
7:30 pm	Tea with family
10:30 pm	Go to bed

Or like this:

5-7 am	Wake up, make the day's resolution, breakfast, ask what good shall I do this day?
8-11 am	Work
12-1 pm	Dine, read
2-5 pm	Work
6-9 pm	Put things in perspective, music, conversation, examination of the day's work, ask what good have I done today?
10 pm-4 am	Sleep

Or a weekly ritual which looks like this:

Monday	Managing and running the company
Tuesday	Product
Wednesday	Marketing and communications, growth
Thursday	Developers and partnerships
Friday	Company culture and recruiting

The first one is a typical day in the life of Charles Darwin. The second contains the daily rituals of Benjamin Franklin.

The third is the weekly ritual of Jack Dorsey, founder of Twitter, where he focusses on specific subjects during each 8-hour workday during a 5-day week.

You will notice that they give equal importance to leisure as well as work, personal as well as professional matters such as family and recreation.

Of course, during Darwin's and Franklin's time, they did not have to worry about email or TV. However, you will realise that when you develop a ritual, you allocate time for the important things in your life.

You decide and choose what you will do every hour, every day, or what to do on which days of the week. You commit to the ritual so that it becomes a regular, repetitive act.

You replace your routines with rituals. You go from being merely busy to being productive. You go from doing transactions to making transformations, within you and around you.

7. Clear the clutter and do more.

Do you find it difficult to make up your mind when offered a choice? Do you prefer to let someone else choose your lunch from a restaurant menu?

When things don't go according to plan, do you panic?

Do you find fault with others? Are you always blaming yourself for not trying hard enough?

Do you get tired easily? Do you mistrust people? Do you often expect the worst?

Anxiety, confusion, depression, feelings of fatigue, inability to concentrate, distractedness or pessimism—these could all be the result of the clutter surrounding you.

How can a desk littered with paper affect your disposition? Or a bag full of knick-knacks? Or a closet filled with too many clothes? Or how can a room in a state of disarray affect your productivity?

You'll be surprised how easily you can distract someone's concentration by just tilting a picture frame on the wall or pulling your necktie askew.

When you are surrounded by clutter, it can affect your behaviour.

Your mind mirrors your environment.

Have you noticed how people behave when they talk to each other in a loud and noisy environment? They are easily excitable, agitated or even irritable.

Put a person at a construction site, in a factory, a workshop or even a night club for just a few minutes and they will show some kind of behavioural change. They will start talking loudly or gesture wildly or simply show signs of distraction.

Now, imagine a person who spends a whole working day in a place that is filled with noise and visual clutter. You cannot expect that person to be at his or her productive best. They may be trying to do their best but unfortunately they cannot sustain their focus.

Success results not only from your efforts but is also influenced by the environment that you work or live in. Look at the desks of people who are consistently good at their work and you will find order.

Music or noise, which do you prefer?

I have a police detective friend who has a peculiar habit. I can usually tell when she is working on a complicated case. Her office suddenly looks spick and span.

I can run my finger on any surface and not find a speck of dust. Everything is squeaky clean, from the floor to the surface of her desk.

She says that tidying up her office and putting everything in its proper place helps her mind to focus. Invariably, she cracks the case while she is doing something totally unconnected like wiping the windows or watering the plants.

My friend says that order is like music. It has a soothing effect on your mind.

Clutter, on the other hand, creates chaos and is like noise. It disturbs your concentration and prevents you from being productive.

My friend has more than once demonstrated that getting rid of clutter and tidying things up energises the mind. It allows her to think clearly and focus on the right kind of things.

5 key benefits of being neat and tidy.

1. You gain more time for productive work.

Back in the earlier days when a computer slowed down, you may have heard of a maintenance task called defragmenting. This typically involved putting the blocks of data stored on your drive in a sequential order. Nowadays, most operating systems automatically perform this function.

The point is you should have a system or process of putting things in their proper place after you pick them up and use them. For instance, in a warehouse, items are stored in a particular order so that despite a huge inventory of goods you can find anything in no time.

When your environment is usually neat and tidy, then you will immediately see the effects of it in your work. You will find that you get things done faster and more easily.

Otherwise, you may be spending a lot of time and effort rummaging for things amid the chaos

2. You can focus more on the important stuff.

Less is more. It's true. You can be more successful when you have less stuff around you to distract you.

When Mark Zuckerberg, Facebook founder was asked why he wore the same grey t-shirt every day, he is reported to have replied that he wanted to clear his life so that he had to make as few irrelevant decisions as possible.

Getting rid of such sartorial choices as what to wear, according to him, enabled him to focus on more important stuff such as how best to serve the community. Other examples of this are Steve Jobs in his black turtleneck and jeans or Barack Obama, usually seen in almost identical-looking suits.

3. You can reduce or eliminate stress.

Clutter comes between you and the life you want to live. When you visit a museum or an art gallery, take a look at the faces of the people around you. You will find that most of them appear to be calm and serene.

That's because the neat and tidy environment of an art gallery or a museum is reflected in the minds of the people who visit these places. The same applies to any place where things are neat and tidy such as a ballet studio or a library.

4. You save money.

When you are organised, you will not spend money unnecessarily on buying the same things. Duplication may seem like a very minor issue but how many times have you bought replacement batteries for a device and discovered a pack of the very same batteries in your bottom drawer? Or bought another copy of the same book because your bookshelf is not organised?

It's like making multiple duplicate copies of the same file in your computer. It unnecessarily takes up space and slows down the computer.

5. You are safer.

How come there are fewer aircraft accidents than automobile accidents? This is simply because the skies are less crowded than the roads. Accidents happen mostly when there is chaos. People who work in cluttered workplaces often suffer from allergies or other breathing ailments.

Most of these chronic health conditions are triggered by dust, mould, fungi and other unsavoury particles lurking around in dark, dank corners of unhygienic work environments.

You can see a clear improvement in your productivity by just getting rid of the unnecessary stuff around you. However, remember that clutter is not merely physical; it can also be mental and emotional.

So, trying to focus on too many things at a time or trying to please all the people all the time can also affect your productivity. We'll look at these in detail, in the next two chapters.

8. Identify the time-parasites.

"Hey, do you have a few minutes?" said Peter, "I am meeting a new client and I thought it would be a good idea if you could join us."

Of course, the meeting goes on for about an hour. You knew from past experience that it was going to be a waste of time. By the time you get back to your desk you realise that you could have simply said no.

~~~~~~~~

"I am sorry, I got delayed. I thought you might be late as well. Have you been waiting long?" asks Stephanie.

You shrug, smile politely and lie, "I've been here a while but it's alright."

You've been waiting for almost half an hour and it's definitely not alright. You were almost ready to leave when she walked in.

~~~~~~~~

"You should have joined us for drinks yesterday evening after work. We had a blast. Do you know what happened?"

He goes on to tell you something about last night's antics, followed by a joke and then shares a bit of gossip about the new intern.

He goes on and on and you can't get in a word edgewise. You point at your watch, then at your computer and make some more frantic gestures with your hand.

"Oh, you've got to be someplace else?" he asks.

"No, I've got work to do," you say.

He still sits there yakking away and you pray for realisation to dawn upon him that you are not interested in his anecdotes.

~~~~~~~~~

You may have experienced something similar to the situations described above. Despite your best efforts to make the most of your time, you will come across people who will prevent you from doing so.

These are the time-parasites. While they don't suck blood, they are no less dangerous. They suck your time and by the time they're done, you have lost those precious moments forever.

They leave you frustrated, and given enough time, they can even turn you into one of them.

Do you want to turn into a parasite?

All kinds of people make up the world. There are people who do things or get things done. They are the doers.

Then there are those who will have something to say about everything but when it comes to action, they slack off.

The doers may not pay much attention to the slackers but the latter will not lose any opportunity to divert the former from their work.

Then there are the interrupters. They'll make some inane comment when someone is saying something important or even worse, doing something. It's either an attempt to justify their own existence to themselves because they know they are not doing much or they just like to hear the sound of their own voice.

Perhaps they are afraid that no one will notice them if they don't interrupt and so they throw in a hammer when the wheel is spinning.

Beware the drone bee.

Then there are those who are very busy or they seem to be. Well, they are usually busy wasting other people's time. They call for meetings but rarely turn up on time.

Did you know that there are three kinds of honey bees in a hive? There's the queen bee, then there are the worker bees and the drone bees.

The worker bees are the ones which flit about from flower to flower gathering nectar. They make honey. (Is it just a coincidence that honey sounds so much like money?)

The drone bees make a lot of noise especially when they are around the hive which is almost all the time. The point of their existence is to mate with the queen bee and so they do not have much else to do most of the time. So they just buzz around the hive.

It's not very easy to tell a drone from a worker bee. They are almost similar in appearance and differ only in their actions.

You may come across many busy-bee kinds in the corporate and business environment.

When you see a busy-bee kind of a person who talks a lot, is always calling for meetings and appears important, it's easy to get taken in and think that they are really doing something worthwhile or important.

They are generally always in some meeting or another and you wonder when they get any work done. You really wonder if they get any work done at all.

You realise that these time-parasites cannot survive without wasting someone else's time. They cannot do anything on their own.

They are the ones who usually tout the importance of team effort and take credit for work that someone else does. They need nice guys who are polite and will not say no to their time-sucking activities.

They will barge in on your time and space and say something like, "Hey Bob, can I pick your brain?" and simply expect you to drop everything and listen to them. Why?

They do it because they want to show you that they are doing something important because otherwise they are worried nobody will ever notice.

5 ways to rid yourself of time-parasites.

1. Identify who they are

This is the first step. Make a list of people you know who have let you down in the past. You can try to block their number or not answer any calls from them. If that's not possible, then you can be prepared and when they call or show up, tell them you cannot indulge them or that you are busy doing something important.

More often than not, time-parasites take you by surprise and take advantage of your good nature. If you identify them, then you are alert to the danger they pose. This helps you to prevent them from sucking up all your time and therefore you can stop them from encroaching upon your space or time.

2. Use the scarecrow method

Scarecrows are essentially harmless but they are very effective in keeping pests away. I once saw a girl at a crowded café do something very interesting.

She took out a book from her bag, opened the book and took out a piece of thick paper, obviously a bookmark. She folded the bookmark into a tent and placed it next to her cup of coffee. It was a bright red bookmark which had the letters "DO NOT DISTURB" written in bold white letters.

If you have a door to your workplace, then you can close it and hang a DND sign on the knob. If you work in an open office environment, then you can do what this girl did. Place it on top of your desk or stick it on a placard and attach it to your PC, desk or chair. Just as effective is putting on large and obvious headphones, even if you don't listen to music, you can happily ignore everyone else as you pretend you can't hear them.

3. Learn to say no

When someone interrupts you or asks you to do something you don't want to, decline politely but firmly. This also goes for any online meeting invitations which you don't want to attend or you foresee as a waste of time.

A simple way to find out if a meeting is going to be worth your while or not, is to look at the agenda, if there is one. You will be surprised how many meetings don't seem to have any real or plausible agenda.

If there is no agenda, then ask for one, and most often you will be able to tell if it's going to be a waste of time or not.

4. Avoid vampire nests

Most time-parasites move in circles where they can flourish. In any typical office, you'll find them frequenting the water cooler, the coffee machine, the meeting rooms, the smoking area and such places. You can simply avoid them by staying away from these places.

5. Protect your space

You can actually define and defend your work space from time-parasites. You can specify certain times of the day when you will not entertain visitors or phone calls.

If someone comes and hovers around your desk or sits on your desk, you can politely tell them you don't have time for whatever it is they want to discuss. Over time you will notice that when they are being consistently ignored, they will stop bothering you.

If you think dealing with time-parasites is tricky, then there is a whole other tribe of gremlins which are even stealthier. They are not roaming at large but live within you.

In the next chapter, we look at the multitasking myth and how trying to do too many tasks at the same time can fritter away our time and make us lose our focus.

9. Do one thing at a time.

At a job interview, the hiring manager tells the candidate, "This is a high profile position. You will be expected to play multiple roles and handle multiple responsibilities. Why do you think you are best suited for the job?"

"I am great at multitasking," replied the candidate. This was the response the interviewer was looking for.

Do you find yourself answering your emails while talking to someone? Talking to someone on the phone and checking your online messages is one thing but many people do this even while talking to someone face to face. And it's not even considered rude but required.

The test of a computer's efficiency is how quickly and easily it can switch between applications. When you have multiple applications open on the computer system, if there is a noticeable delay or if the computer stalls, then it's considered not to be efficient enough.

The same principle is applied to people. Should it be?

Multitasking is expected.

If someone is writing a report and the phone rings, then the person is not expected to stop doing what he is doing to attend to the call.

Instead, while answering the call, he or she will cradle the phone in the crook of their neck while continuing to type. On the other hand, if the person stops typing to answer the phone, then he is losing time and thus being inefficient. Don't you find?

Ours is the age of multitasking. Teenagers are texting while watching TV. Mothers are talking on the phone while feeding the baby. Doctors are doing the same while examining a patient. Chefs are doing it while cooking.

Multitasking is not just expected but celebrated.

Is multitasking a strength?

"I can only do one thing at a time. Let me finish what I am doing and after that I'll look into it." Anybody who says something like this is considered to be old-fashioned, inefficient or slow.

However, the myth of multitasking being considered to be a desirable quality is based on the assumption that doing two or more things is better than one.

Apparently, people who do more than one thing at a time are good at it. At least that's what we thought or liked to believe, until recently.

Two studies conducted in 2009 and 2010 raised some doubts about the merits of multitasking. A Stanford researcher asked 262 students to do some experiments that involved switching between multiple tasks, filtering information and using their memory.

It was naturally expected that multitaskers would outperform non-multitaskers. Surprisingly, they found that multitaskers used their brains less effectively than non-multitaskers.

In 2010, tests conducted by a research agency in France showed that when a person attempts to do two tasks simultaneously, the brain divides its resources to attend to each task. Naturally, this results in a lack of focus. The person's concentration is impaired and the possibility of error increases.

Why do road traffic regulations not allow a person to use the phone while driving? It divides the driver's attention and thereby increases the likelihood of causing an accident.

It was found that 23% of automobile accidents in the US in 2011 involved use of a cell phone. The driver was distracted because he or she was either dialling or talking or texting using a mobile phone while driving.

Are we straining our brain?

When we constantly switch from one task to another or attempt to perform multiple tasks at the same time, the level of dopamine in our brains increases.

Dopamine is chemically responsible for making us feel happy.

So, in effect multitasking makes us happier, at least in the short-term. It's similar to the rush a gambler feels when he is playing a game of chance.

However, along with Dopamine, multitasking also triggers the release of adrenaline and other stress hormones. What we fail to notice or recognise is that while we are doing two things, we are not concentrating.

It is found that the information we receive when we multitask is not easy to retrieve. So if a person has been talking to someone while typing a report, it becomes increasingly difficult for the person to recall all the things that were discussed on the phone.

This is exactly what happens when we answer our online messages while in a meeting. Our ability to recall things or process information suffers. Our brains become less efficient due to chronic multitasking.

Not only are we not paying attention to the points being discussed in the meeting, our sense of reasoning is distracted and so our responses to the emails may not be exactly what we wanted to say.

Why do something with half a mind?

In a court of law, cell phones are switched off. Why? They can interfere with the proceedings and it could lead to an unfair judgement because the jury or the judge is distracted.

In an auditorium, during a play or an opera, the audience is requested to switch off their mobile phones. Why? It can distract the performers and also mar the enjoyment of the performance by the audience.

Bruce Lee once said that he was not afraid of the man who has practiced a thousand different kicks but the man who has practiced one kick a thousand times.

When we multitask, we lose the one thing which is most important to achieve excellence, and that is focus. Rather than divide our attention, wouldn't it make sense to do one thing at a time?

Mindfulness improves productivity.

In the Japanese Zen tradition, they have a saying which describes the tea ceremony, "Ichi-go, ichi-e" which roughly translates to mean "One time, one meeting."

The story goes that the founder of the Japanese Way of Tea was once asked what the most important aspect of the ceremony was. He replied by describing the whole process from making the tea, to keeping it warm and serving it with consideration.

Many people failed to understand the meaning or significance of what the Zen master was saying. His answer implied that doing even the simplest things with mindfulness makes it a productive use of our time.

According to Zen philosophy, it's not worth doing anything if you don't do it with full presence of mind. This ancient wisdom of mindfulness is worth invoking especially now in this busy and modern age when we mindlessly and automatically try to do more.

Does multitasking really make us more efficient? When we switch between tasks, don't we switch between different faculties of our brains? Don't we in the process lose time and therefore lose our productivity?

Isn't multitasking complicated? Isn't it why we get stressed? Isn't it why we make mistakes? Is it worth the effort?

Finally, let's ask ourselves if we really enjoy multitasking? Does it truly make us happy? Do we really become productive? Or are we just doing it because everyone else is?

10. Do more with a 50-minute sprint.

"I can sit there and do nothing as good as anyone," says Margaret, one of the characters in the movie, *Clockwatchers*. She couldn't have been more right.

A person can spend the entire eight hours in an office sitting at his or her desk and still fail to be productive. We all know that despite the 9 to 5 routine or the stipulated 8-hour workday, productivity does not happen just because employees show up for work.

On the other hand, a person can work from home, or from anywhere for that matter, and still productively contribute to the organisation they work for.

Do you find this hard to believe? Well, there's a bold new breed of business leaders who do.

Ditch the desk.

The founder of Facebook, Mark Zuckerberg, doesn't have a desk or an office. Nor does the company's COO, Sheryl Sandberg. They usually use one of the many huge conference rooms at the company's headquarters in California.

Daniel Ek, CEO of Spotify doesn't have a desk. He has often been spotted sprawling around on a couch like a teenager doing his homework.

Scott Heiferman of Meetup is another CEO who doesn't have a traditional private office or desk. He has been seen many times sitting in the lounge area of the company's headquarters or temporarily sitting at the desks of other employees when they are not there.

If you think it's a trend only found in the technology industry, then it is not. Art Peck, the CEO of clothing retail company, Gap Inc., does not have a desk.

These are successful entrepreneurs, visionary business leaders and consistently productive people. If they are doing something which is obviously working for them then why shouldn't it for everyone else?

Many organisations such as the Gerson Lehrman Group, a New York consulting firm with over 250 employees does not believe that productivity comes with a desk. According to Business Insider, GLG gives its employees a locker, a laptop and the freedom to roam around the office and work from anywhere including an in-house coffee bar.

Are you stuck at your desk?

Don't work hard or for long. Work smart. We've heard this advice many times and yet most companies still consider it important that their employees punch in and spend 8 hours at a desk in the office.

Are they being productive during this period? That's another matter altogether.

There is increasing evidence to show that sitting at your desk for long periods is not only unproductive but also unhealthy. The human body was not designed to sit for a long time and work at a desk.

Studies show that when you stand, stretch, walk, run, move and do anything other than sit, you can see a remarkable increase in your

58

productivity. Even meetings conducted while walking and talking have been proven to produce better results than sitting and talking.

When you sit, no matter how ergonomically well-designed or comfortable your chair or desk is, your brain becomes sluggish after a while. It is not as active as it is when you are walking or even standing.

It's simply a matter of breathing and blood circulation. When you stand or walk around, your spine is erect and you are breathing much more deeply. As we know the intake of oxygen has a direct and positive effect on our blood circulation.

Our brain functions better as a result of the optimised blood flow making us more focussed, more alert, quicker in our responses and thereby more productive.

What's the ideal productivity period?

It was clear that working at a stretch for one hour or even many hours does not increase productivity. If a person finds that he is not feeling energised or motivated after a period of continuously working, then he or she should take a break and go for a walk or stretch or just do something else which does not involve work.

When they come back, they will feel much more energetic. People who take breaks in between work have been found to produce better results than those who don't.

We already know about this from when we examined the Pomodoro Technique in Chapter 5. The technique demonstrates how we could maximise productivity by interspersing relaxation breaks regularly in between working periods.

So, how long is the ideal productivity period? Is it 30 minutes or an hour? It is a pertinent question to ponder over so as not to spend too much or too little time on a particular task.

After all, underutilising the ability to focus on a task could be as detrimental to productivity as stretching it.

The answer is 52 minutes of productivity followed by 17 minutes of relaxation, according to a study conducted by the Draugiem Group, a social networking company working out of Latvia. The company used the popular productivity app DeskTime to monitor the work habits of its employees.

The time-tracker in the app was used to determine how long the company's most productive employees spent on a task without taking a break.

A clear pattern of working for a 52-minute period followed by a 17-minute break was noticed to be the most productive way to work.

Time your tasks.

A significant insight from this study is that productivity can be improved when you set a time frame for a certain task. Instead of trying to drudge on and complete a task, if you set a timer or an alarm for 50 minutes and stopped working as soon the timer went off, you could get better results.

(While the exact peak productivity period is 52, for practical purposes, it makes sense to round it off to 50.)

You may not always complete the task but the sense of purpose that the time frame imparts enables you to use the time allocated in an efficient manner. The 50-minute time frame also creates a sense of urgency and builds up the pressure of meeting a deadline.

It prevents you from dilly-dallying. It helps you focus with purpose.

Similarly, when you take a break, don't think about work or your next task. Just do something which is not associated with work which will help you relax.

It's important not to be self-conscious about appearing to laze around because that's exactly what you should be doing during your 15 or 20-minute break.

Entrepreneurs should stop behaving like employees if they want to make any real difference. They should stop looking over their shoulder trying to impress or gain the approval of the world.

Employees on the other hand should start performing like entrepreneurs. Instead of pretending to work all the time and putting in long hours to impress their manager, they should practice the 50-minute productivity sprint.

When your productivity improves, appearances don't count. Look around you and you will notice that the most productive people are those who seem to get things done effortlessly.

The secret lies in the 50-minute productivity sprint followed by a break for 15 to 20 minutes.

It is important that during the 50-minute productivity period, you create the ideal work environment. This means that you ensure that there is nothing that breaks your concentration.

In the next chapter, we look at some simple yet effective ways in which you can stay focussed.

11. Focus; Avoid distractions.

Have you noticed the blinkers that racehorses wear? These small square patches of leather covering the sides of a horse's head prevent it from getting distracted from all that's going on around it.

A horse can see pretty much everything around it, from the spectators in the stand to the other horses galloping beside it. Nature intended the horse to have peripheral vision, so they have their eyes on the side of their heads.

While this is a big advantage in the wild where it alerts them to animals that want to prey upon them, it is pretty much a handicap on the racecourse. Wearing blinkers enables the horse to focus on the racetrack and the race.

They help the horse to run as fast as it can. They also prevent a horse from getting distracted and running helter-skelter instead of staying on the racetrack.

Do your best and do it fast.

Similarly, working in any environment generally poses many different kinds of distractions which can cause unnecessary delays and prevent a person from completing a task on time. Not only do distractions cause delay, they can also affect the quality of the work or the output of the person performing the task.

There are many ways to control the distractions around you. You can take personal precautions to prevent them or you can invoke the rules or conventions in an environment to reduce the distractions.

So for instance, a tennis player with long hair will use a hairband to tie his or her hair and prevent it from getting in his eyes and spoiling the line of vision. Similarly, the rules of the tennis court dissuade spectators from speaking out loudly or making any noise when a player is getting ready to serve the ball so as not to break the player's concentration.

In the same fashion, if a student wants to study quietly, he or she can go to the library and be assured that they will have what is often called 'quiet time' to study.

The importance of 'quiet time' or time to work on your own to improve productivity is increasingly being recognised in the modern workplace.

How does teamwork affect time and productivity?

Productivity is often linked to personal habits and the ability to manage time. However, this focus on individual productivity often ignores how a team of professionals collectively manage their time.

In her book, *Finding Time*, Leslie Perlow, a Harvard Business School professor, describes how she found that members of a team ended up working long hours and weekends because of interruptions at work.

An experiment was conducted where 'quiet time' free from any kind of interruptions was introduced three mornings in a week. This not only increased productivity but also drastically reduced the amount of time that the members of the team worked on a project.

By introducing a system which reduced or eliminated some of the common interruptions, the team was able to significantly reduce the time to market required to design, develop and launch a new product.

Find your own time.

Whether you are working in a team or independently on a project, it is important to find an island of isolation that will sharpen your focus and improve your productivity.

Since most of us work using computers, digital distractions are some of the most common forms of interruptions that stall our work and steal our time.

There are many apps available which offer to help you stay focussed on a task. They minimise or eliminate digital distractions by preventing you from checking your email or by blocking social networking websites.

However, even a very low-tech approach can essentially help you to successfully create an island of isolation to concentrate and get things done on time.

William Shockley, inventor of the transistor, is reported to have locked himself in a hotel room for several days to work on his invention. He came out of his self-confinement only when he had completed all the groundwork required to produce the transistor.

This single-minded approach to creating an undisturbed haven to work in paid off for Shockley. He won the 1956 Nobel Prize for Physics.

Making time is different from managing time.

Another great inventor and genius, Steve Wozniak, describes the importance of finding your own quiet time and creating your own individual haven of productivity.

In his autobiography, *iWoz*, the Apple co-founder gives us a glimpse of how great work gets done when you have the best of both, quiet time and an isolated island to concentrate.

He says, "Most inventors and engineers I've met are like me—they're shy and live in their heads. They're almost like artists. In fact, the very best of them are artists. And artists work best alone—best outside of corporate environments, best where they can control an invention's design without a lot of other people designing it for marketing or some other committee. I don't believe anything really revolutionary has ever been invented by committee...I'm going to give you some advice that might be hard to take. That advice is: Work alone...Not on a committee. Not on a team."

In a business world where creative collaboration and groupthink gains favour with management as opposed to independent thought or individual idiosyncrasies, the words of Steve Wozniak echo the spirit of entrepreneurial enterprise.

After all, isn't entrepreneurship all about doing new things and doing them in a way that isn't normal or conventional?

Paul Graham, another great mind of our times, a programmer and a venture capitalist, makes the distinction between what he calls the maker's time or schedule as opposed to the manager's time or schedule.

An individual working on a project is often subjected to the imposition of systems according to the manager of the project. Among other things, this involves attending meetings to interact and share updates on the progress of a project.

While this is important to the manager and the team, it often throws an individual worker's or maker's schedule off momentum. It can potentially upset the flow or rhythm of an individual's concentration which can seriously affect productivity.

Implement individual isolation for productivity.

Acclaimed American novelist, Jonathan Franzen, points out the distractions caused by information overload especially due to technology. These include not only mobile phones, emails and social networking websites but the very design of a laptop or personal computer.

66

Franzen says he prefers working on an ordinary, clunky, utilitarian personal computer rather than a well-designed, sleek and shiny laptop because even the good looks of the machine can be considered a distraction. Franzen is known to go to extremes in order to create an island of isolation when he is writing a novel.

He not only detaches himself from the outside world by cutting off the internet but he does so, literally.

In a *Time* magazine article, he is quoted as saying, "What you have to do is you plug in an Ethernet cable with superglue and then you saw off the little head of it." In all likelihood, Franzen made this comment because he didn't have Wi-Fi on his laptop.

While this extreme approach will guarantee total elimination of any temptation to waste time, it will also make your computer unfit for connecting to the internet, forever. Instead you can implement 'quiet time' and isolation islands temporarily to get your work done on time.

Here are a few tips on how you can achieve this without going to the extreme:

- Work from home for fixed time periods so you can stay in touch with other members of your team while making your own time to work uninterrupted.

- Get to your workplace earlier than others so you can have some peace and quiet before the place starts buzzing like a beehive. Of course, the other alternative is staying back late after work hours but starting earlier gives you the advantage of being fresh and energetic rather than forcing yourself to work when you are exhausted at the end of the day.

- Use noise-cancelling headphones so you can eliminate audible disturbances. You don't necessarily have to listen to music (though music has been known to improve productivity) but use the headphones to block external sound.

- Move away from your desk and work from a conference room that is not being used or even the office cafeteria which is surprisingly quiet in between breakfast, lunch and dinner times. A change of scene has been known to do a lot of good in terms of stimulating creativity and productivity in a person.

- Turn off your emails, take the phone off the hook and put a DND sign on your desk or put on your headphones for specific time intervals during a day or on particular days. This way you can create a temporary 'quiet time' and work without disturbances. However, ensure that you let your manager and team members know about the practice so that there are no misunderstandings.

12. Quantifying Quality.

Would you like to work less and produce more or even better results? Of course, that's exactly what efficiency is all about, isn't it?

One of the biggest challenges that we face in the modern workplace is the use of outdated standards to measure productivity.

Surprising as it may sound, many managers and organisations still view work output in terms of units produced and hours spent rather than value generated.

A hangover practice from the industrial economy, where it was generally profitable to produce more than to produce better, this ethos still influences the way we work today. Despite the exhortation to work smart and not hard, most of us still set store by how much a person works or how many hours he or she puts in.

This is exactly what a recent news report was all about.

It stated that Mark Zuckerberg, the CEO of Facebook spends 50 to 60 hours a week at work.

This is considered to be on par with, or more than most employees at Facebook, or at any other organisation would spend on an average in a typical work week.

Can we quantify quality?

The problem with the report is not that Zuckerberg works hard but that it is considered newsworthy. We still tend to measure a person's productivity not by what he or she produces but by how long he or she works or how much he or she makes.

In the industrial economy, people worked in factories and it was natural to measure productivity in terms of hours spent working. Efficiency meant increasing the volume of output with fewer resources used and in less time.

However, this is not the case in today's knowledge economy. We no longer hire hands but brains. Intelligence increasingly plays an integral role in a company's growth.

Organisations that capitalise on intelligence win, as the new economy has proven time and again. In spite of this, many companies and business managers still continue to think that the best way to increase value is by increasing volume.

It's not just a matter of organisational discipline but also individual approach to work. Most knowledge workers spend on average 41% of their time on discretionary activities which offer little personal satisfaction according to a Harvard Business Review report.

Manage not just time but also tasks.

By focussing only on time management, people tend to forget that one of the important aspects of this is task management.

Mitchell Kertzman, a venture capitalist and former CEO of Sybase, said in an interview, "When I started the company, it was a one-man business. I did every job. I wrote the programs, I sent out the bills, I did the accounting, I answered the phone, I made the coffee.

"As the company has grown, I do fewer and fewer of those jobs. And that's just as well, because I was certainly less competent at them than most people who are doing them now."

Among the reasons why knowledge workers still continue to perform tasks which could easily be done by others is their inability to delegate.

Letting go of tasks that you traditionally performed is difficult unless you make a conscious effort to do so.

People often confuse productivity with being busy. They think everything that they do is important. It isn't.

An Italian economist realised this as early as 1906. Vilfredo Pareto found that 20% of the people owned 80% of the wealth. This inequitable distribution of wealth was also reflected in nature.

He found that 20% of the pea pods contained 80% of the peas in a garden. Similarly, not all the clouds in the sky will produce rain. Only a few will.

You'll find this rule of the 'vital few and the trivial many' across many aspects of work and life.

Are you doing your best?

The 80/20 rule which became known as the Pareto Principle was applied to productivity in the 1940s by Joseph Juran, a management consultant. 80% of a company's revenue comes from 20% of its customers. 80% of the results come from 20% of the people involved. And so on.

If you apply this rule to your individual approach to work, then it implies that only 20% of what you do is really important to productivity.

The difference between doing great work and mediocre work therefore rests on your ability to separate the important tasks from the non-essential or inconsequential ones.

How do you do this?

Prioritise your tasks.

Put first things first, says Stephen Covey. In his list of the *7 Habits of Highly Effective People*, prioritising is the third habit.

The main difficulty with prioritisation is that most people know that they have to do it but they rarely know how to do it. The key to prioritisation is to drop or delegate tasks.

Identify tasks which can be completely eliminated or which can be passed on to others who can perform them as competently as you do them or perhaps even better than you. This is easier said than done. Why?

You cannot focus on two things.

"If you don't prioritise your life, someone else will," says Greg McKeown, author of the book, *Essentialism: The Disciplined Pursuit of Less.* He points out how little we understand what prioritisation means.

"The word priority came into the English language in the 1400s. It was singular. It meant the very first or prior thing. It stayed singular for the next five hundred years."

The need to prioritise or focus on multiple tasks is a malady of the 21st century. It's inefficient but it makes a person busy and therefore it's hard to tell the difference.

Regain your focus. Make time for work that matters. Make meaningful progress rather than multiply your tasks.

Look for and find the value in each and every task. Evaluate a task based on how much value you can contribute. If the task can be outsourced or delegated, do so.

You will soon discover that the pressure of having too little time and too many things to do was merely an illusion. An illusion created by a flawed or distorted way of looking at time management and productivity.

13. Find time for your body, mind and spirit.

Picture a juggler at a circus show. He is juggling three balls in the air. He is doing it almost effortlessly. You can also see that he is enjoying it.

There is a smile on his face and his eyes are dancing as his hands gracefully catch and toss each ball with barely a flick of the wrist.

He is in a blissful state where effort and enjoyment are well balanced.

Now imagine adding another ball to the equation, then another, and another.

The juggler will continue to juggle but with each new ball, his movements will become more frantic, and what was once an energetic and graceful rhythm will turn into a struggle.

There will be a point when the juggler finds one ball too many. That's when all the grace and beauty, the rhythmic movement collapses into a melee of confusion.

The juggler loses control and the balls drop down. This happens at work every now and then.

People shout and throw things. They lose control. They become victims of overwork.

74

Enthusiasm and energy is replaced by despair and fatigue.

Recharge and renew your energy.

Don't allow your work to become burdensome. Find time to relax and enjoy life. You will discover that you can be more productive and happier this way.

It's not enough to take a vacation once in a year. You need to take one every day.

When you find time to exercise, meditate and relax on a regular basis, you will feel more energetic and find the work you do more rewarding. This is so because we only have a limited supply of energy.

When you perform certain activities you expend energy. So you need to balance these activities by relaxing and rejuvenating your mind, body and spirit so that you can regain the energy that you have spent.

Tony Schwartz, bestselling author of the productivity book, *The Way We're Working Isn't Working*, and founder of the Energy Project, tells us that people perform at their best when they move rhythmically between spending their energy and renewing it.

He goes on to tell us about the four kinds of energy that we possess: physical, mental, emotional and spiritual. It is important that we devote time, effort and attention to each of these energy elements in order to lead a balanced and fulfilling life.

Energise your life.

There are two simple ways in which we can energise our days—by exercising and meditating. Alright, I can already hear the excuses: lack of time and motivation.

Saying that you don't have time to exercise is the flimsiest excuse. Think about it for a moment. Are you saying that you can't spare even an hour every day for your mind, body and spirit?

Yes, that's all it takes. You don't have to be an athlete or a fitness fanatic. Just 20 to 30 minutes of working up a sweat can do you a world of good.

The human body is designed to function well only when it has adequate rest and nutrition. Our bodies are not meant to run on caffeine and hot dogs.

We don't build strength by sitting in a chair for 8 hours. We cannot develop a sense of wellbeing if we don't have the strength or the spirit to work.

Sweat to reset.

Exercise makes us happy. Happier people produce better work. This is a proven fact.

How does exercise make us happy?

It's to do with the endorphins and a few other processes that happen in our brains and bodies when we exercise.

Endorphins are a chemical compound that surprisingly, is produced to combat stress. When you start to exercise, the brain recognises this as a moment of stress and releases endorphins.

When you exercise, your heartbeat and your blood flow increases, signalling the brain. Your brain interprets this excitement as similar to what is experienced when you fight or flee from danger.

So along with the endorphins, your brain releases a protein called Brain-Derived Neurotrophic Factor or BDNF, to protect your brain from stress. This compound essentially acts as a reset switch for your physical and mental system.

This is the reason why we feel good after going for a run, or going to the gym. When you work out, you not only expend energy but you also train your system to store energy in a better manner.

Working for long hours can lead to burnout caused by expending more energy than you have. That's why there is a limit to the number of hours a person can work efficiently without a break.

Beyond a certain point, a person is liable to drop the ball when overworked. This can be especially dangerous because it can adversely affect a person's health and also jeopardise their own safety as well as that of others.

Find your focus.

Exercise fortifies your body with the energy to accomplish things. When you are physically fit, you will feel tired less often and therefore be able to sustain your energy for longer and more productive periods of time.

However, physical energy is just one aspect of the equation. Most of the work we do in the knowledge economy requires us to be mentally alert.

The importance of meditation in keeping your mind and spirit in fine form is equivalent to exercise and nourishment for the body. The reason why many people hesitate to consider meditating is because they associate it with something that is very difficult to do.

This erroneous assumption may be the result of equating meditation with sitting cross-legged on the floor in an uncomfortable position and chanting mumbo-jumbo. This picture of meditation is not at all correct.

Meditation may not be easy at first but neither is it as difficult as you may think. It is simply a matter of spending some time contemplating your thoughts and finding focus.

We are used to being constantly plugged into different forms of media, whether it is reading a book, listening to music or watching TV. We may therefore find it strange or rather unsettling to actually sit still for a few minutes, seemingly doing nothing.

This is essentially what you need to do when you start meditating.

It helps to learn how to meditate by attending a course. Thanks to the internet, you can do so without leaving your home. You can download and read a book on how to meditate, or you can watch a video online that demonstrates simple meditation techniques.

Find a state of flow.

Having a hobby or going on a holiday also helps a person to relax and recharge energy. A hobby which you enjoy can help you appreciate the benefits of meditating.

Engaging in an enjoyable activity such as a hobby puts a person in a state of flow where they are completely engrossed. This is an excellent way to relax, relieve the stress of everyday work and recharge your energy.

The state of flow was first described by a Hungarian psychologist, Mihaly Csikszentmihalyi in 1975. Csikszentmihalyi studied the habits of artists and creative people who went into an almost trancelike state when they were intensely focussed in an activity.

It was observed that thought, action and awareness merged when a person was in a state of flow.

Csikszentmihalyi described the state of flow as, "Being completely involved in an activity for its own sake. The ego falls away. Time flies. Every action, movement and thought follows inevitably the previous one, like playing Jazz. Your whole being is involved and you're using your skills to the utmost."

Practising meditation is somewhat similar to having a hobby. When you are in a state of flow, you also find true happiness which is not dependent on the outcome of your actions. You find your action and the moment of time when you are doing it intrinsically rewarding.

After all, if you are happy, then all your efforts make sense. Otherwise, what's the point of being productive? We explore more about the connection between happiness and productivity in the next chapter.

14. What makes you tick?

Are happy people more productive? Or does productivity or success make people happier?

The answer is obviously yes to both questions.

How can a company or an organisation contribute to enhancing the happiness of its employees? Will offering regular pay increases, a better work environment, better work-life balance or more benefits help? It seems reasonable to believe so.

At the same time, it makes sense to believe that success in an endeavour or being consistently productive will create happiness in a person. The complex connection between happiness and productivity has been the subject of various studies. Let's examine some of them.

How does happiness influence productivity?

A team of economists at the University of Warwick in the UK conducted some experiments to explore the relationship between happiness and productivity.

One group of people were shown a funny video featuring a popular comedian. They were also offered fruits and chocolates while watching the movie.

Another group were shown a neutral video which didn't have any emotional content. People in the second group were given no refreshments.

Following this, both groups were given similar tasks to perform. People in the first group were found to be 10-12% more productive than those in the other group. This goes to suggest that the immediate environment, external stimuli and inducements can influence both happiness and productivity.

In his book, *The Happiness Hypothesis*, Jonathan Haidt points out that people were reported to be found happier before they achieved their goals rather than after. If the pursuit of happiness is a hamster wheel, then the point of it is not so much about getting somewhere as it is about enjoying the run.

In other words, success does make you happy but not so much as happiness makes you successful. To mimic the chicken or the egg question, which comes first, happiness or success?

It is in a person's best interests to consider happiness leading to success rather than success to happiness. Why? It's possible to create a subjective sense of happiness whereas the best we can do before we achieve success is to visualise or imagine it.

What's the face value of a smile?

In one of my businesses, there was a colleague who hardly ever smiled. Everyone was generally chirpy, at least in the mornings when they came to work, exchanging good mornings and meaningless banter but not Carl.

He always had a blank look on his face and acknowledged a greeting with a nod rather than a smile. I could not understand why he was so unhappy.

Other than that there was nothing wrong with him. He was alright with his work but did it with hardly any emotion.

He was an average guy. However, is that what you want to be? Do you want to be just average or do something extraordinary?

In another study, the economists at Warwick examined how real-life incidents such as the death of a family member or a friend or an illness affected a person's happiness.

Participants in the study were asked to rate their happiness levels. They were also asked to indicate the cause for it. Following which they were asked to perform certain tasks.

As expected people who said they were unhappy were less productive than those who considered themselves happy. Therefore, is happiness subjective?

Negative incidents in your life can and will affect your happiness but only if you allow that to happen. It is natural to feel sad when you suffer a loss but it is neither healthy nor practical to brood over it. It will affect your productivity.

Can you create happiness?

Happiness is a state of mind. If you think that you are happy, then you are. Your happiness depends on what you think and believe in.

If you think that your happiness depends on certain conditions, then you need to make those conditions happen in order to be happy.

Most often the conditions are social, professional and financial. Happy people value relationships. They help other people and are also willing to accept help from others.

They recognise the importance of a rewarding career and a reliable source of income. However, they are not workaholics or obsessed with making money. They also value their time and want to make the most of it.

You have the right to be happy. You also have within you the power to be happy. It doesn't matter whether you are an employee or an entrepreneur, whether you work in a team or you work on your own.

You can influence your happiness and also the happiness of the people around you. You may not be able to control the outcome of your actions but you can positively influence how you go about achieving your goals.

If you want to do something, just wishing for it isn't going to be enough. You have to plan and put your plans into action to make your wish a reality.

If you want to be more productive, you can start by enjoying what you do or change what you do and find something that you will enjoy.

If you work with people who are not emotionally invested in their work, then find out how you can motivate them. If not, help them relocate and replace them. Perhaps they are not happy doing what they are currently doing.

Would you be happy working with a person who is not productive? Similarly, would you be able to be at your productive best if you are not happy?

Make time not money.

Our time on its own is worth nothing. It's what we do with our time that matters and creates value.

As simple as this may sound, happiness is linked to finding meaning and purpose in what you do. It is not enough to do something just because it pays the rent.

How does your work affect your wellbeing? How does your work contribute to the happiness of others?

Does your work excite you? Do you think what you do will make a difference to the world?

Every time you want to do something, ask yourself if it is worth your while? If you don't then you could end up becoming someone like Carl.

You could do an average job and get paid for it but you will enjoy neither the work you do nor the fruits of your labour. Making money and then spending it to buy stuff may not necessarily make you happy.

However, making time for the things you want to do will. Spending your time doing what you like will make you happy. Spending time with people you cherish will contribute to your happiness as well as theirs.

It's your choice.

A successful salesman once told me that the secret to closing a sale lies in the customer. He said it doesn't really matter how deep a salesperson's product knowledge is or how good the price offering is, if the salesperson does not like the customer.

The key to closing a sale is to like the customer as a person so that you can establish a connection. When you show that you like someone, the person automatically tunes into your wavelength, trusts you and believes in your sales pitch.

When you know that you like your life, you smile. Otherwise you frown. Happiness does not happen at random. We have the choice whether to be happy or not.

We cannot control unfortunate or negative incidents in our life that may cause unhappiness. We can choose to count our blessings or ignore them.

A happy person is therefore in control of his or her disposition. If you want to make the most of your time, then you should stop brooding over the past or worrying about what the future holds.

Be present in the here and now, and you will discover that it doesn't take much to be happy.

15. Don't try to do everything.

In one of the earlier chapters, we looked at the Pareto Principle which indicates that 80% of the results come from 20% of the efforts. This implies that a majority of what you are doing may consist of discretionary tasks or those that you could delegate.

Why delegate? Besides the multiple benefits of being able to improve your productivity, delegating enables you to claim back your free time.

Though gaining free time may sound like an anomaly when we are trying to improve productivity, it isn't. We often confuse being busy with productivity.

When you are busy, you don't get the time to do or think about the work that really matters to you.

Therefore, you fritter away your time doing inconsequential tasks while ignoring the really important ones.

When does work becomes drudgery?

"I perform better under pressure." How many times have you heard someone (or yourself) say this as if it is something to be proud of?

Do you realise that being overwhelmed by work is not only bad for productivity but it also prevents you from enjoying your work? Instead of giving into the demands and pressures of work, have you considered easing out your schedule so you can be more relaxed?

If your answer is no, then is it because a sense of guilt prevents you from making it easy for yourself? Do you think that by pushing your limits and keeping yourself constantly engaged, you will do better work?

Are you afraid to take it easy and relax while at work? Do you worry about not appearing to be busy?

"The really efficient labourer will be found not to crowd his day with work but will saunter to his task surrounded by a wide halo of ease and leisure. There will be a wide margin for relaxation to his day. He is only earnest to secure the kernels of time, and does not exaggerate the value of the husk."

This is a picture of how you should approach work so that it becomes meaningful, according to the American philosopher and poet, Thoreau. Work becomes drudgery when you fill your schedule with urgent but unimportant tasks.

Why do we race round the clock?

If you are running around trying to get too many things done, then it is more likely that you will do most of them poorly. We are constantly putting our time and efforts at the mercy of the tyranny of the urgent.

The urgent will always seem important because you are not able to look beyond the immediate in your haste to complete the work. The really important work gets hidden by the myriad urgent tasks that you crowd your schedule with.

This is also known as 'busy work'. It makes you busy or at least makes you look that way. 'Busy work' is not really productive work.

Sometimes 'busy work' is work which is easy. You may be keeping yourself busy by doing easy tasks so that you don't have to take on the difficult ones.

The irony is that while a person appears to be busy, he or she may actually be shirking their responsibilities or slacking off from doing the real work that they are supposed to do.

"I am busy doing this and this and this. Once I finish these tasks, I will look into that."

Does this sound familiar? Doesn't it sound like an excuse? Doesn't it sound like 'busy work'?

How to free your schedule from the tyranny of the urgent? First of all, find out what truly makes you happy. Find out what part of your work is a labour of love.

You have to learn to differentiate between 'busy work' and work that matters.

Separate these from the rest. Then see how much of the urgent, the unimportant and the busy work you can delegate. If you can't delegate, then outsource.

Why is delegating difficult?

The primary impediment to delegating is often your own attitude to work and your apprehensions about delegating. You fear that by delegating you will lose control. You may also be afraid that by delegating, you may render yourself dispensable or without much to do.

Face your fears and put them in perspective. Delegation does not necessarily mean abdicating responsibility or completely letting go. When you delegate a task to a co-worker, you can still keep the lines of communication open so that you are aware of the progress of the task.

Don't demean yourself by thinking that your worth is determined by the small tasks that you think you need to do. Only when you free yourself from these, will you be able to focus on the important work.

Michelangelo could have spent his time making tombstones out of marble. He chose not to. Instead he focussed his energy on building immortal works of art.

You can also raise your work to the level of art. Make it meaningful. Free yourself from getting bogged down by the urgent. Measure your time and productivity in terms of how much satisfaction you derive from doing it.

Delegate, don't duplicate.

Remember that the point of delegating a task is to enable you to allocate and use that time for something else which is important. Therefore, it is necessary that you clearly establish the role and responsibility of the person to whom you will be delegating a particular task. Define objectives to be followed and standards that need to be met.

Don't delegate and then continue to focus on the task. It is a waste of time and resources if two people end up doing the same job

Provide guidance and training if necessary to the person to whom you are delegating. Make sure the person has or acquires the skills and competency to perform the task.

Show confidence in the person's ability to do the task and refrain from micro-managing the task. Inform other people who are involved in the work about the delegation so that they are not surprised.

Expect errors at least in the beginning and give freedom to find solutions. If you are delegating to a co-worker or subordinate, and a problem arises, the person may turn to you for advice.

This is called upward delegation. The person you delegated the task to, constantly seeks approval or supervision from you at every stage of a task. Don't duplicate a task that you delegated by redoing it or checking or supervising a task which somebody else is clearly responsible for.

Resist the urge to solve a problem yourself. Instead encourage the person to find the solution on their own. This builds confidence and a sense of responsibility.

Be patient and avoid spending time on the very task that you delegated. This will only complicate things and contribute to increasing your work instead of reducing it.

Connect to professionals worldwide.

Outsource, when you cannot delegate. What's the difference between delegating and outsourcing?

Delegation is possible normally within an organisation, where a co-worker can take on the responsibility of completing a task or tasks.

Outsourcing generally refers to using the professional services of an individual or company outside the organisation. Especially for entrepreneurs and start-up companies who are bootstrapped in terms of resources, outsourcing offers great opportunities to get the work done competently as well as cost-effectively.

The internet has made it possible for even the smallest enterprise to go global. You can easily connect with a worldwide talent pool of professionals to assist you in reducing your work load.

Any task that does not require a person to be physically present in your office location can be outsourced. Some of the commonly outsourced activities include office administration, accounting services, legal, designing, writing, editing, translation, technology, programming, sales and marketing as well as engineering and manufacturing. (For more ideas, see my other book *The Art of Entrepreneurial Outsourcing—100 mission-critical roles you can outsource).*

Whether it is hiring a virtual assistant or a designer to develop a website, you can easily search for and find freelance professionals who can remotely do it for you. And usually, at a fraction of the price you would normally pay if you hired someone locally.

There are many websites which offer the professional services of freelancers with a proven track record. So it is as easy as or even easier than hiring someone locally.

Doing business long-distance is no longer difficult. In fact, you can turn it to your advantage. We'll explore more about this in the next chapter.

16. Commuting. Avoid it or use it productively.

People in the US spend on an average 1 hour every day commuting to and from work, according to recent statistics. Around 20% of these are mega commuters or those who spend 90 minutes or more on the road.

Studies show that when a person's commuting time increases, the less healthy and less happy they become. People who commute for longer hours also feel more stressed and less well-rested than those who commute less.

A Swedish research discovered that if one person in a marriage commutes for more than 45 minutes a day, then the chances of the couple divorcing increases by about 40%.

To put it mildly, commuting is not good for you. As a matter of fact, commuting is more often than not a total waste of time. Almost everyone who commutes knows this.

Then, why do people commute?

Why not live close to where you work?

The usual reason that most people give is that they cannot afford to live close to where they work. So they follow their real estate agent's advice and drive further and further away from the city until they can find someplace that they can afford.

However, this is most often only half the story. A primary incentive for living away from the city is to have a better quality of life. Or at least, that's what most people believe.

The location of a house or apartment is dependent on many factors considered more important than the person's workplace. In fact, proximity to the workplace is often the least important.

Space or size of the apartment is one. You can definitely get a bigger apartment or house for the same money or even less, the further you move away from the city centre.

Pollution, both air and noise, is another important factor. Proximity of schools, family members, hospitals, parks, shopping malls and other facilities for essential and recreational activities also play integral roles.

Reduce your commute and reclaim your life.

Most people think about affordability when they spend their money. They consider the value they are going to get when they buy something.

You should do the same with your time, especially your commute time. Are the advantages of living far from your workplace really benefitting you? Can you really afford to spare the time spent in commuting?

You only have a finite number of hours in a day. If you spend more than an hour in commuting to and from work, then it's time you started examining your priorities.

Add up the number of hours you spend every week and calculate how many hours are spent in a month. Now, consider the option of reducing that time by a quarter or a half. Will you be gaining at least 10 hours a month? Imagine the things you could do in that time.

Could you claim back 3 days or a week in a year if you reduced your commuting time?

How can you reduce your commute?

The first option, of course, is to consider moving to a house or apartment that is closer to your workplace. You chose to live further away because you believed that your and your family's quality of life would be better.

Ask yourself and your family if this is true? Is living so far away and commuting to work making you happier? You will discover that finding out the answer may not be easy or obvious but it is worth asking.

The second option is to propose a flexible work arrangement with your manager or the HR department of your organisation. Before you discard it as not practical, find out if working from home is an option.

Check if it is possible to do it on an experimental basis for one day in a week and then increase it to 2 days. Every little time that you can reclaim by reducing your commute time counts.

The output and results that an employee produces is more valuable to a company than face time or showing up at the office. The nature of most jobs in the knowledge economy is that they don't require physical presence or supervision as they did in a factory during the industrial economy.

Technology has made it convenient and easy for managers to communicate with as well as supervise a remote workforce. Many small and medium enterprises are deliberately hiring people who are willing to work from home.

This is a growing trend. A company can function from a smaller office if most of the employees work from home and thereby significantly reduce overheads. Employees also save on commuting time as well as travelling expenses.

Work is no longer location-dependant.

Telephone calls, videoconferencing, online work platforms that enable sharing documents and files in real time, laptops and other mobile internet devices have separated work from the desk.

An employee is no longer required to sit at his desk to be productive. In fact, as we have seen earlier, people are inspired to produce better quality work when they have the freedom to choose where and when they work.

Even small and medium enterprises as well as start-ups are finding it increasingly easy to go global. They no longer have to limit their search to the local talent pool. A whole world of opportunities (in terms of talent resources) is available to those who are willing to look beyond their geographical territories.

People in a company are increasingly working in a virtual environment and collaborating as effectively as if they were sitting in the same office. A designer in Barcelona collaborates with an engineer in Bengaluru to develop a product for a company in California while the product is manufactured in Chongqing.

The advantages of creating a virtual work environment actually go beyond both the organisation and the employees. It's good for the environment as well.

Less commuting means less pollution and less traffic congestion, as well as less road rage and fewer accidents.

Turn commuting to your advantage.

Combine reducing your commute time with making the most of the time by using it productively. The easiest way to do this is to catch up on your reading.

There's a wide choice of reading material and it's readily available online. From newspapers to business magazines as well as ebooks, you can read them all online on a tablet or an ereader.

The advantage of reading online is that you can decide what you want to read spontaneously instead of carrying a particular newspaper, magazine or book.

If you are driving to and from work, then consider audiobooks or podcasts. Instead of listening to the radio or the same kind of music every day, you will find that you can increase your knowledge or even learn a new skill or language by listening to an audiobook.

Finally, if you have been able to reduce your commute time measurably, consider using a healthier and more environmentally-friendly mode of transport.

Instead of driving to work, how about cycling? Or if you live close enough, try walking. This way, you will get the benefit of the exercise, while making the most of your commute time as well.

Walking or cycling to work also gives you an opportunity to detach yourself from work and regain focus. Make your commute into a moving meditative practice by focussing on your breath and your thoughts.

17. Detach digitally.

A best-selling author of business productivity books was returning home after a speaking assignment. On the flight, in the seat next to him was a businessman who was checking his emails on his laptop.

It was obvious he had recognised the author. The businessman thought it would be a great opportunity to strike up a conversation.

The author had other plans.

"This is a 7-hour flight and I wish to use it to rest and relax. So instead of talking to you for half an hour or so, I can offer you a lot more. I'll give you about 10 years of my life."

He pulled out a copy of his latest bestselling book and asked the businessman, "Have you read this?"

The businessman shook his head and said no. The author said, "I'll sign this and give it to you but on one condition. You will turn off all your electronic devices and not use them to check your emails or connect to the internet during the journey."

The businessman thought this was a strange request but he thought about it, saw no harm in it and agreed.

The author asked his co-passenger his name, then took out his pen and wrote, "To John Smith, Thank you for your wonderful company on the

98

flight from New York to London." He autographed the book and gave it to the businessman.

For the rest of the journey, they didn't say a word to each other. The businessman was engrossed in reading the book, while the author did practically nothing other than eat, sleep and read a novel or a magazine when he was awake.

The author wanted to use the journey as an opportunity to do a 'digital detox'. This meant disconnecting from information streaming through the internet via any electronic device. If the person sitting next to him checked his emails, then he realised he may be tempted to do so himself.

Are you digitally dependant?

Look around you and you will notice people constantly consuming information through different forms of digital devices.

They may have earphones plugged in and will be listening to music or some other form of audio streaming in through their smartphones or mobile media players. Whether they are sitting and having a coffee, or strolling by or purposefully crossing a street, the ubiquitous wires trail from their ears.

Or they may be interested in what's going on in other parts of the world or in other people's lives while being unaware of what's immediately happening around them. I once saw a couple at a cafe, seemingly on a romantic date, sitting next to each other peering into their respective smartphone screens.

The only time they spoke to each other was to share something that they found interesting online and then to take a selfie. I could imagine them reading the steady feed of information coming through their social networking site or a news website. I wondered why they didn't just sit at home and chat with each other online.

Relationships are not the only casualties of internet addiction and information overload. Our cognitive abilities can also be severely impaired due to an overdependence on digital devices such as smartphones or tablets.

Do you take your phone when you go to the bathroom? Do you carry your phone while going for a jog or while working out at the gym?

Every time your phone pings or beeps signalling an incoming instant message, do you immediately reach out for it? Do feel that your phone is ringing even when it is not? This is called 'phantom ringing', a curious phenomenon affecting the digitally dependant.

Are you constantly communicating with people via chat or instant messaging? Do face-to-face meetings make you uncomfortable?

You may be suffering from a severe case of digital dependency. What you need is a digital detox.

Even the most productive people digitally detox.

"When you go on a holiday, your routine is interrupted; the places you go and the new people you meet can inspire you in unexpected ways. As an entrepreneur or business leader, if you didn't come back from your vacation with some ideas about how to shake things up, it's time to consider making some changes.

"I make sure that I disconnect by leaving my smartphone at home or in the hotel room for as long as possible—days, if I can—and bring a notepad and pen with me instead. Freed from the daily stresses of my working life, I find that I am more likely to have new insights into old problems and other flashes of inspiration," said Sir Richard Branson while expressing his views on the importance of taking holidays.

Though the founder of Virgin Group did not explicitly mention the words 'digital detox', he obviously was referring to the danger an overload of digital information can cause. Our over-dependence on the internet and smart communication devices can prevent us from using our minds as we normally would for inspiration and creative ideas.

The former Chief Technology Officer of Cisco, Padmasree Warrior also makes it a point to stay away from technology, one day in a week. She turns off her smart phone, doesn't check her emails or voicemails and completely ignores the internet on Saturdays.

She says, "A few years ago I found I was working all the time—entire Saturdays and Sundays—to the point where I wasn't being creative and I felt like I was not making the right decisions. I was focussed on the quantity of what I was doing rather than really making quality decisions."

Here's Tony Schwartz, CEO of the Energy Project and a bestselling author, describing a plane journey. "I'd brought along a pile of books, mostly novels, and none of them related to work. I began reading and very quickly became absorbed."

How to digitally detach?

If some of the most prolific and productive people in the world think it's worth digitally detaching, then shouldn't we all take a cue from them?

I take five to seven days every two months to sort out the 'brain noise' of day-to-day decisions. I go to a silent retreat where I can meditate with no phone, internet or computers to distract me. The absence of the need for even small talk helps me to collect my thoughts, refresh my mind and rejuvenate my spirit.

This may be a bit intense for most people but a holiday works as well. You work hard for what? Isn't it so that you and your family can have a wonderful life? When you are on holiday, don't take work with you. Turn off your phone so you are disconnected from work.

One bad email can stress you out for the rest of the holiday. Whatever problems may arise at work in your absence, you can deal with it when you return.

Or you can set aside a day in a week (or a month if that's difficult to start with) where you will resist the urge to connect with any of your digital devices. Turn off your smartphone. If you are worried about any messages you may miss, then put your phone in airplane or flight mode.

Do not turn on your computer or tablet. You can even turn off your modem.

Talk to the people in your life. Have conversations with your family members. Invite friends over for a meal.

Resist the urge to update your status or take pictures and post them on social media. Read a newspaper—not a digital version but a real one. Read a real book not an ebook.

Most important of all, do not turn on the TV (more on this in the next chapter). If you are bored, don't fret. Just stare into space and do nothing.

All this may seem counter-productive but when you go back to your digitally-connected world, you will feel refreshed and rejuvenated.

Our constant need to be in touch with the world through technology can be a stressor and prevent us from being in touch with our immediate environment. Our connection to people and events far from us can distance us from our near and dear ones.

Switch off digital devices and turn on your mind. Detach yourself from technology and feel free. Stop checking time on your digital devices. Let time flow freely. Reclaim your time and your freedom.

18. Turn off or throw away the TV.

"How much time do you spend watching TV?"

When people whine about how busy they are and how little time they have for themselves or their family, this is the question you should ask them.

You'll be surprised to know that rarely or never will any of them reply saying, "I don't watch TV." Yes, there really are people in this world who say they don't watch TV but we'll come to that in a bit.

When people say they don't have enough time to exercise, what they often mean is that they'd rather watch TV than exercise. One of the most common things we see in households today is people sitting around having dinner while watching TV.

Having a meal used to be a social occasion. It was an opportunity to have a conversation with your family and friends. You break bread and you talk. Now we shush people when they talk because we don't want to miss what's happening on the TV screen.

If this isn't pathetic enough, people perform tasks mindlessly while watching TV. I have seen a person at the gym turning on the TV without fail every time before she gets on the treadmill. It's as if she is conditioned to run only if she can watch TV.

I know another person who irons his clothes while watching TV. Then there are the people who have a TV in their bedroom. It's not the only TV they have. No, they have a bigger TV in their living room and a smaller one in the kitchen.

Get rid of your TV or turn it off. There's no simpler way to stop wasting your time and reclaim your life. If you realise you don't have enough time in the day, then simply stop watching TV.

Are you in control?

Don't get me wrong. I don't hate TV. I like TV just as much as the next person. I do watch TV but now I do it with a certain degree of discernment. I care about when and what I watch on TV.

The old joke goes that the person who has the TV remote control is the person who has the upper hand in a home or a family. The joke's on you if you believe this to be true.

We hardly have control over anything when we have the TV remote in our hand. We can switch channels if we want to but do you realise how much time we end up wasting while browsing channels? Then again you may not really like any of the programmes on any of the channels.

If you spend two minutes every day (and that's a conservative estimate) browsing channels, that's an hour every month and a whole day every two years. Apart from this, there are the commercials which, whether you watch them or not, still waste your time. In every hour you watch TV you will come across 10-15 minutes of advertising.

They don't call it the idiot box or the person watching it a couch potato for no reason. Studies indicate that most of the content on TV slows our brain functions.

Even people who were casual TV viewers when asked to stop watching TV displayed withdrawal symptoms similar to what drug addicts go through when they stop taking drugs. In an experiment, people were offered a monetary incentive to give up watching TV for a year.

Most people who participated in the experiment preferred to forego the financial rewards rather than give up watching TV.

According to a report, the average American spends over 5 hours a day watching TV. If you calculate that, it amounts to over 2 months in a year! Imagine what you could do if you had 2 extra months every year?

Well now you can have them if you want to.

Turn your TV off.

If you say that you watch only educational programs on TV, then you better listen to what Groucho Marx said. "I find television very educating. Every time somebody turns on the set, I go into the other room and read a book."

Turning off the TV is a great way to reclaim your time.

If you wish to take control, then turn off the TV once in a while. Similar to having a digital detox day, have a no-TV day every week.

Reclaim your life.

Is your life built around the TV programme schedule? Do you tell your friends that you cannot go out on Tuesday because your favourite show is airing?

Do you reschedule your dentist appointment to watch the finals of a game or match on TV? Are you delaying your need to go to the toilet till a commercial break appears?

Haven't you heard of Netflix?

Watch what you want, when it suits you.

Similarly, you don't have to put your social life on hold or delay your visit to the bathroom or the dentist. Instead of watching a show when it airs, why not just rent it and watch it online when it is convenient, pause and play when you want?

106

Don't let the TV rule your life and waste your time. Do what a growing number of smart people are doing.

Turn off the TV or tone down your viewing habits. Better still, get rid of the TV.

You will not be alone. You can count yourself among some of these famous people who said they don't own a TV or they don't watch it.

Mark Zuckerberg wrote on his Facebook page, "Is there a site that streams the World Cup final online. I don't own a TV."

"I don't own a TV. I listen to music or read books or see friends," said Keira Knightley. Alan Cumming is another actor who doesn't own a TV.

Madonna also says she doesn't watch TV. Jesse Eisenberg also says he doesn't own a television.

Isn't it strange that most of these people appear on TV but they themselves don't watch it? Don't you think they might have some sound reasons for doing so?

Angelina Jolie is reported to have said, "I don't watch TV and I wasn't reading anything. So I started writing." So there you go, not watching TV may even get your creative juices flowing.

Novelist Chuck Palahnuik, author of *Fight Club*, said, "I haven't had a TV in 10 years, and I really don't miss it, because it's always so much more fun to be with people than it ever was to be with a television."

That brings us to one of the oldest and most enjoyable ways to make the most of your time. Spend your time with people, which is what we talk about in our final chapter.

19. Eat with family and friends.

People who have an active social life are healthier. The number of friends you have and the number of times you meet them can contribute to your health as much as giving up smoking or exercising regularly.

These encouraging views about our social habits were the result of different research studies that explored the connection between our eating habits and health. It was found that it is not just enough to eat nourishing food but it is equally important how you ate and with whom.

Do you do other things while you eat such as watching TV, checking emails or texting from your phone? Do you generally eat alone or do you socialise when you eat?

Eating food while watching TV can cause indigestion or lead to other long term health complications such as obesity. When we eat, our stomach sends signals to our brain when we have had our fill or feel sated.

If we are watching TV, the brain is distracted and we usually tend to overeat. We also do not relish or pay attention to what we are eating and therefore all food tastes the same and even delicious dishes seem insipid.

People who live in the islands of Okinawa in Japan and the residents of Sardinia in Italy are some of the happiest and longest living people on earth.

Researchers delved deep into their food, eating habits, work and lifestyles to find out what were the factors that contributed to their happiness and longevity.

They found that not only did the Okinawans and Sardinians eat a healthy and well-balanced diet consisting of food which they mostly grew but that they also ate their food together with others. They shared not just the food but the joy of eating.

They did not eat alone or while they were doing something. They treated their mealtimes as an important ritual in their everyday lives.

Mealtimes were devoted to not just food but conversations with family members and friends. They maintained close-knit relationships not only with family members but also neighbours and guests.

Eating is a celebration of life.

Historically meals have contributed to creating our social, cultural and even religious traditions.

Every meal provides an opportunity to talk and discuss subjects honestly that people would otherwise feel hesitant to talk about.

This could perhaps be because eating helps us to relax and we are much more emotionally connected as well as psychologically relaxed or have an open mind during mealtimes. In almost all cultures and religions, celebrations and festivals revolve around a meal.

Whether it is the American tradition of Thanksgiving, the Christian festivals of Easter or Christmas, the Islamic celebratory feast of Eid or the Jewish Chanukah, the meal plays a significant role in the celebrations. Just as important as turkey is to Thanksgiving, potato pancakes are to Chanukah.

Similarly, the festival of Kwanzaa is recreated in America along the lines of the harvest celebrations of Africa with a dinner table laden with fruits and vegetables. On New Year's Eve, the Chinese eat noodles signifying longevity.

You can turn every meal into a celebration by eating it with family and friends instead of eating alone. How we eat may also contribute to our attitude to work and pleasure.

You often hear people who are busy say, "Let's grab a quick lunch and get back to work," or they simply skip a meal. There may be exceptional days when you are actually busy and doing so may be alright.

However, if you do this regularly, then it's time you considered if you have got your priorities right. We work so that we can nourish our body, mind and soul.

If we do not have time to do even this, then what's the point of all the hard work? Poor is the person who does not have enough time to spare to enjoy a meal.

Although they may have all the riches, they are still poor because they don't have time.

Eating enhances intimacy.

Food is almost always shared. Whether it is among members of a community or a family, food has traditionally brought people together.

When people gather at the dinner table, food almost assumes a symbolic role. It's not just for nourishment alone but for social bonding and interaction that we eat together.

People go out on a date to a restaurant. Yes, some people would go out for a movie but which would you consider as a more romantic environment: a restaurant table with candlelight or a dark movie theatre where you have to stare straight ahead, instead of into the other person's eyes?

Does a person read the newspaper at breakfast so that he or she doesn't have to make conversation? Do we take our dinner plates and sit in front of the TV so as to avoid talking with other family members?

When you invite friends over, do you want them to sit and watch TV while they enjoy a meal? Or would you rather sit across the dining table and have meaningful conversations?

Get closer by eating together.

As the saying goes, the family that eats together stays together. Don't dilute the importance of mealtimes by eating in front of the TV or using your phone to answer a text message or check your social media feed.

As important as eating is the preparation. It is convenient and easier to order a pizza once in a while but not always.

As humans, we are the only living beings on this earth who cook their food. This is one of the significant differences between us and animals.

We started cooking our food so that we could feed our increasing intelligence. Wouldn't it be foolish if we ignore the very method of preparing our food which makes us who we are?

So it is important that we share this ritual of cooking as much as we share the practice of eating. Encourage everyone to share in the preparation of a meal, whether you are having a simple poolside barbecue or an elaborate multi-course meal.

Even children can lend a hand and learn about the importance of cooking a homemade meal. Let them cut the vegetables or stir the soup as it simmers.

You may not be able to have a sit down dinner every evening but can't you arrange to do so at least once or twice in a week?

Similarly, renew your social connections by not merely liking their posts or tagging their picture but by actually talking to one another over a meal. You will discover that some of the most memorable moments you will cherish will be the conversations you have over a meal.

You can either be busy or you can make time to spend your mealtimes with the people who matter. The choice to build a wall of busyness around you or build a network of social connections is up to you.

Cherish every moment and relish every morsel. Make the most of your time on earth by making every meal and every moment count.

So, instead of saying, "Let's grab something to eat on our way," how about saying, "Let's meet for dinner," or "Let's do lunch." You will live healthier and happier. You are also guaranteed to have a great time.

Don't let time fly by while you are busy. Make it linger while you have a great time.

Summing up

There will be times when you are working and there will be other times when you are not. There will be times when you need to be alone and there will be other times when you need to be around people.

This book is as much about managing your time as it is about living your life to its fullest possible potential. So don't let time fly away. Have fun while being at your productive best.

The 19 ways to do so are summed up below. You don't have to apply them in the order that they are described nor all of them all at once. Practice one at a time.

1. **You have time but not just for you.** Leave no room for regrets. Give yourself, your goals and your relationships equal importance. Strike a balance between your work and your life, your career and your family.

2. **Start. Now.** There is no time like the present. Overcome procrastination and get started with the work you've been putting off. Take the first step and stop being afraid of going on a journey.

3. **Write your 'not-to-do' list.** Take a fresh new look at one of the most popular productivity principles. Make a list and make it

work by identifying and eliminating activities that waste your time.

4. **Schedule your day the night before.** Apply the advantage of advance planning to your daily life. Wake up feeling fresh by giving sleep its due importance. Use the Daily Priority Sheet to make every movement and moment in your day count.

5. **A tomato now and then will get things done.** Put into practice the Pomodoro Technique. Take breaks between your productive periods to get your work done with ease.

6. **Replace your routines with rituals.** Instead of doing mindless chores, practice acts of conscious choice. Let what you used to do by force of habit make room for productivity that's driven by deliberate desire.

7. **Clear the clutter and do more.** Mess creates stress. Get rid of the unnecessary noise that clutter creates and prevents you from being productive. Discover the manifold benefits of keeping your life neat and tidy.

8. **Identify the time-parasites.** Get rid of the people who waste your time. Learn and apply foolproof ways in which you can protect your space and time from these monsters.

9. **Do one thing at a time.** Stop straining your brain by multitasking. Prioritise and focus on single tasks. Start streamlining your time. Make mindfulness a practice to overcome daily distractions.

10. **Do more with a 50-minute sprint.** Time your tasks and take breaks in between your ideal productivity periods. Get maximum mileage for your efforts and from every moment you work.

11. **Focus; Avoid distractions.** Stay focussed by implementing 'quiet time'. Learn to create your own 'islands of isolation' and achieve unparalleled peaks of productivity.

12. **Quantifying Quality.** Separate the essential from the unimportant. Apply the 80/20 law of the Pareto Principle to improve productivity. Manage your tasks along with your time.

13. **Find time for your body, mind and spirit.** Prevent your work from becoming a burden. Energise your body with exercise and your mind with meditation. Don't drop the ball. Learn to be in a state of flow.

14. **What makes you tick?** Happiness and success are interconnected. Find happiness in what you do or change what you do. Enjoy the journey without waiting to arrive at the destination.

15. **Don't try to do everything.** Drop the tasks that turn work into drudgery. Delegate what you can and outsource the rest. Get rid of 'busy work' that crowds your time. Make room for quality instead of quantity.

16. **Commuting. Avoid it or use it productively.** Go location independent. Get creative with your commute time. Reclaim your life. Leverage technology to connect without commuting.

17. **Detach digitally.** Turn on your mind and tune out from technology for a while. Find some respite from the brain noise created by your daily attachment to digital devices.

18. **Turn off or throw away the TV.** Get yourself unstuck from the screen. Stop scheduling your life around the boob tube. Recover your time and discover freedom by turning off the TV.

19. **Eat with family and friends.** Enjoy one of the oldest social traditions. Have stimulating conversations over a meal. Strengthen your social connections in a deliciously delightful way.

An accomplished entrepreneur and speaker, with a career spanning several industries, Craig D Robinson has used outsourcing in all his businesses to leverage the power of people, without the huge cost.

One of his most notable outsourcing achievements was to generate a 570% increase in quotes for his construction company, whilst saving 11% in the estimating department.

Craig is passionate about wellness and adventure. He has completed several trail ultra-marathons, is a qualified skydiving instructor and an avid adventure racer. He stays focused and balanced by spending 7 days in silent meditation every 2 months.

A Father, volunteer firefighter, philanthropist and owner of multiple businesses, Craig also finds time to volunteer with children who suffer from disability and is the founder of a Social Enterprise to help refugees start and run their own businesses.

Craig also consults with a wide range of companies, specialising in creating and implementing systems to outsource mission critical roles.

To connect with Craig, visit www.craigdrobinson.com

www.ingramcontent.com/pod-product-compliance
Lightning Source LLC
Chambersburg PA
CBHW070255190526
45169CB00001B/422